P9-BZC-988

CUZ

CUZ

OR THE
LIFE AND TIMES
OF
MICHAEL A.

DANIELLE ALLEN

LIVERIGHT PUBLISHING
CORPORATION

A Division of W. W. NORTON & COMPANY
Independent Publishers Since 1923
NEW YORK   LONDON

This is a work of nonfiction. Certain names and identifying
details have been changed.

Copyright © 2017 by Democratic Knowledge, LLC

Printed in the United States of America
FIRST EDITION

For information about permission to reproduce selections from this book,
write to Permissions, Liveright Publishing Corporation, a division of
W. W. Norton & Company, Inc., 500 Fifth Avenue, New York, NY 10110

For information about special discounts for bulk purchases, please contact
W. W. Norton Special Sales at specialsales@wwnorton.com or 800-233-4830

Manufacturing by LSC Communications, Harrisonburg
Book design by Barbara M. Bachman
Production manager: Anna Oler

ISBN 978-1-63149-311-9

Liveright Publishing Corporation,
500 Fifth Avenue, New York, N.Y. 10110
www.wwnorton.com

W. W. Norton & Company Ltd.,
15 Carlisle Street, London W1D 3BS

1 2 3 4 5 6 7 8 9 0

For my Aunt Karen, and the millions gone

Temptations, hidden snares, often take us unawares.
And our hearts are made to bleed for a thoughtless
   word or deed.
And we wonder why the test when we try to do our best.
But we'll understand it by and by.

—**GOSPEL SONG**

CONTENTS

I

RELEASE AND RESURRECTION

Limits are
what any of us
are inside of.

—CHARLES OLSON

1.

GARDEN PARTY, July 2009

"Danielle, phone call for you. It's your dad."

I broke away from a conversation with my husband's cousins—from glancing, distracted talk about the kids who were playing yards away in their floral sundresses under a soft English garden-party sun. Rising from the picnic table, I took the cell phone from him and walked a few steps.

"Hi, Dad."

"Danielle, it's Michael."

My father's voice, the careful, clipped speech of a retired professor, came from across the Atlantic, from Maryland through the ether, but sounded as if it were miles beneath the seas, crackling, wispy as if through the first ever transatlantic cables.

"He's dead."

"*What?*"

"Dead. They found him shot in a car."

"What?"

"Dead."

"I'm coming."

Michael. *My* cousin. My baby cuz.

Sometimes on English spring mornings a gauzy haze clings to the air. This, though, was July and, now, afternoon, but that same sort of whiteness suddenly seemed to wrap the sky and the surrounding willows, and I near collapsed, staggered into my husband's arms, and said "Jim, we have to go."

"What?"

"Michael's dead."

"*What?*"

"Dead. We have to go."

Straightaway go, we had to go, to South Central.

And so we left.

2.

Three years earlier, I had arisen one Thursday morning well before dawn. I was in my palm-tree-shrouded vacation condo in Hollywood, California, feeling the most glorious sense of anticipation I have ever known. It was June 29, 2006. I was still married to my first husband, not Jim the philosopher from Liverpool and second husband, but Bob, the professor of poetry who had grown up in Hollywood in the 1950s and '60s.

As I wended my way past the kidney-shaped pool and climbed into the old white BMW I'd bought from my mother, my spirit was filled with a light, almost sweet buoyancy easy to savor in the Southland quiet of that June day. Strange to admit, but even when my first child was born some years later, the anticipation was not so simply blissful. Waiting with Jim for Nora's arrival was an experience shot through with fear and joy. Resurrection, it turns out, is more transcendent than birth, or so it was then, as I headed to my aunt's small stucco cottage on a block in South Central where a few doors down, on the corner, a fortified drug house stood like a hostile sentry. Her house appeared serene. It was always reasonably neat, if also in a state of disrepair, and as the sun rose over the tidy, pale houses, it colored them pretty. Poverty never looks quite as bad in the City of Angels as it does in the winter-beaten Rust Belt.

My aunt Karen, my father's youngest sister, the baby of a set of twelve, now herself forty, was about to drive a crew of us to collect her own baby, her third child, Michael, from "Reception and Release" or, as it is called, "R&R." Prison life is rife with black humor.

I was along. So was Michael's "Big Sis" by eighteen months, Roslyn, and one of Roslyn's own babies, Michael's eight-year-old nephew, Joshua. We were on our way to collect the last son of an extended clan, youngest child of the youngest daughter.

If I had it to do over again, to meet another loved one on his day of liberation, I'm sure the fear would now overpower the joy. It's not that, on a rational level, we didn't know how hard reentry is, how low the probability that any given life turns a corner. But to know something intellectually is so very different from feeling it in your flesh, straining after some goal with every fiber of your being only to sink in the end to defeat.

Everyone was looking forward to a homecoming party for Michael. In the driveway of my aunt's house, next to the postage stamp of a lawn, uncles and friends, cousins and second-cousins, and cousins once or twice or—who knows—how many times removed, would pull folding chairs up to folding tables covered with paper tablecloths and laden with fried chicken and sweet tea. I was eight years old when Michael was born. My guess is that he was probably the first baby I ever got to hold and I had grown up with him. The baby of a sprawling family too numerous to count, he was also *my* baby, a child of magnetic energy and good humor.

We had lost him when he hit fifteen, eleven long years ago. He had been gone from us almost half his life. Now he would be with us again.

Today, though, we were just going to collect Michael and see what he wanted to do. We would drive to the parking lot by Tower 8, not the normal Tower 2 location for visitors. There we would wait until the white van drove up to deposit those prisoners being released. We were to arrive by 8 A.M. sharp, no exceptions. From L.A., in the early rush hour, it could take us as much as two hours. But once we arrived, we would have to wait. Possibly an hour. Possibly half the day. No one could say in advance.

The drive seems like something of a haze. I remember a wait, but I don't think it was, in the end, terribly long. We all sat—nerves taut—in the car. And I remember somehow being in a green and shady grove, which made the experience altogether different from every other trip to Michael's last prison in Norco, a little, dusty stretch of Riverside County just south of the unfurling black ribbons where the 10 and the 15 freeways join.

It's a cliché to say that someone has an electric smile, but what else can you call it when someone beams and all the lights come on? Michael arrived and smiled. His broad, toothy grin, gums and all, always seemed to take up half his face, a bright flash of white against his dark skin, and he always had a little bob in his step that you could recognize as belonging to the playground athletes of your youth. He had that natural spring as a child, even at every prison visit and, to be sure, on this day of his release after over a decade of incarceration.

His late adolescence and early manhood were, like those of so many millions, gone behind bars, and nonetheless he bounded toward us. How could we not sing hosannas, and think, "God is great"?

His mother, deep brown and plum-cheeked, warmhearted and big-chested, wept, or so I believe. "All things work together for the good," she might have said, as she often does when thinking about Michael's story. Again, these are details I just cannot recall.

Then we came to asking him what he wanted to do. Fulfilling that request would be my job, as would helping him in the months to come through reentry. Not mine alone, no, but mine consistently—day-after-day as the cousin-on-duty, the one with resources, the one whose parents had been to college, and who was expected to go to college, and who had done so, and who had turned into a professional.

I was ready. Or at least I thought so. Like a coffee klatch of nervous first-time parents, we had all been preparing for months—my father, the retired college professor; my aunt, the nurse; Michael's older brother and sister, each struggling to make ends meet; my husband, Bob, the poetry professor, himself near retirement; and me.

We did have plans, but they were not the plans we had hoped to have. Michael had been working as a firefighter for the last few years. He loved the work. He should have been paroled to a fire camp or to a fire station. We even had family in Riverside County. They were ready to take him. He could have lived with them and gone to school and kept on pushing back and beating down wildfires.

But the rule was, you had to be paroled to the county where your crime was committed. In his case this was Los Angeles County. Need I add that L.A. County is crime-ridden? We didn't have the plans we had hoped to have because of this policy on parole, but we had developed the best alternatives we could. As the Secretary of Defense who got us into the Iraq War once more or less said, we were going to have to go to battle with the army that we had.

Step one was this: on the way back to L.A. County, ask Michael what he wanted to do first.

Michael wanted to buy underwear.

3.

THE INVESTIGATION,
July 2009

After my father's phone call, we left the party immediately, so I don't know if the willows ever stopped swaying. While the earth itself settled back into its more reliable wobbly orbit, we booked our plane tickets to Southern California and tried to figure out what was going on. No one knew much. The best anyone could do was direct me to a few news items gleaned from the Internet.

Headline No. 1, from KTLA:

BULLET-RIDDLED BODY FOUND IN CAR

LOS ANGELES—A body riddled with bullets was found inside in a car in South Los Angeles, police said Saturday. Police responded to a call of a suspicious person sleeping in a vehicle in the 1000 block of West 60th Street at around 5:20 P.M. Friday, said Officer Rosario Herrera of the Los Angeles Police Department. On inspection, officers discovered the sleeping man propped up in the car's passenger seat was really a bullet-riddled body wrapped in blankets. The body was identified as that of Michael Alexander Allen, 29. Allen suffered multiple shots to the torso, Herrera said. Police have no motive or suspects in Allen's shooting. Anyone with any information on the shooting is asked to call the LAPD Criminal/ Gang/ Homicide Unit at (213) 485-1383 or (877)-LAPD-24-7.

These were the basics. One didn't know how he died, or how he'd ended up in the car. About his corpse, however, there was information to be found in a Los Angeles Police Department blog.

Headline No. 2:

MAN FOUND DEAD IN CAR

LOS ANGELES—The Los Angeles Police Department needs the public's help to identify and locate suspect or suspects who fatally shot a 29-year-old man on July 17. Yesterday, at around 5:20 P.M., a patrol unit from 77th Division was dispatched to the 1000 block of West 60th Street. The radio call was generated in response to a report of a suspicious vehicle with what appeared to be a person sleeping inside. When the officers arrived they found Michael Alexander Allen, a 29-year-old male Black, wrapped in bedding on the passenger seat. He was pronounced dead at the scene. The vehicle and victim were transported to the Coroner's Office where he was taken out of the car.

Did the police hoist the "vehicle and victim" onto a flatbed tow truck, or winch them on behind and pull them, a yoked pair, along the road? Did passengers riding in cars alongside witness a seemingly "sleeping" man? The gods must chortle every time death's chariot, like Charon's ferry, pulls up in the form of a rusty tow truck. This is too routine a feature of death in America, in our blood-spattered culture, this image of the dead being hauled off as "evidence," the most basic human ritual of ministering to and caring for the deceased interrupted.

Yes, of course, it makes more sense to invite the next of kin not to a street corner but to the coroner's office to claim the victim's belongings. Yet the rawness of the rough concrete curb at 60th and Vermont, and the grimy adjoining gutter that paralleled the road's black asphalt, was surely a more suitable cauldron for the smelting of grief than any coroner's antiseptic office. And when one thinks of Michael now, one never thinks first of the clickety-click wheels of a coroner's efficient bureaucracy but of this corner, whited-out with urban despair. Here, smack on the corner of Vermont and 60th, belong the gnashing of teeth and rending of veils.

As we waited to fly across an ocean and continent, Karen and her daughter, Roslyn, Michael's "Big Sis," went to claim his few, forgettable belongings. The little hatchback appeared to have bloodstains on the floor of the passenger's seat, but my cousin, Roslyn, also struggling with poverty, so needed a car that she would soon claim it as her own all the same.

4.

GETTING STARTED,
June–July 2006

Michael's homecoming party was grand. Spirits were light. The merriment went on all afternoon and seemed to attract some attention from the neighbors. More than once the same glamorous-looking woman drove past, ever so slowly, in a fancy, low-slung, two-door golden brown Mercedes sports car.

After the party, we got down to business pretty quickly. Michael did spend a certain amount of time eating favorite foods—Doritos, fried chicken, and his sister's homemade mac and cheese. He played Football Manager with eight-year-old Joshua and other nephews and nieces who had been born while he was in prison. But he wanted to make something of himself. He had flourished as a firefighter in prison. He was ready to find something to do again, to create a life, a span of action of which he could be proud.

Neither of us had time to waste. Eight years older than Michael, I was telecommuting that summer from L.A. to my job as dean of the Division of Humanities at the University of

Chicago. Having started school at the age of four, I'd never left, and one year earlier, at thirty-two, I'd been appointed one of the youngest top administrators in the university's history. Despite a generous and supportive provost for my boss, I could manage the job from afar only so long. My age was already reason enough for people to wonder whether I could master the work. I didn't want to let the provost, or his boss, the president, down. I couldn't afford to appear to slacken my focus. The pressure of my job would limit my time with Michael.

Michael and I made task lists—my usual tactic for all things personal and professional—and we moved through them efficiently. We met the parole officer, a woman Michael thought was tolerable, and we figured out the routine. Or rather, I waited outside in the driver's seat of the ten-year-old BMW 325. During those early days, I was the willing chauffeur. In fact, I would never meet Michael's parole officer. Now, years later, I realize he wanted to keep me separate from his life as a convicted felon. He wanted to show me only the other side, the part of him that could have gone to college.

From the parole office we went to the bank, and Michael opened an account. Then it was the library, where I went in. These places were, after all, my turf, and under my watch Michael got a library card and started learning how to use the computer. At last, as we began searching for jobs, Michael met Google, which hadn't existed when he went to prison.

Next up was the driver's license. Although Michael had driven trucks as part of his work on the inmate fire crew, he'd never had a license. He'd been arrested when he was fifteen and didn't leave the prison system for eleven years until he was twenty-six. He loved cars and now, finally, he was going to get a license, so the DMV had to come immediately after the bank and library. I drove him there and waited outside while he took the test. He passed easily, which was no surprise.

Then we started the job hunt in earnest. Everywhere we saw a HELP WANTED sign, Michael filled out an application. This meant a lot of places. These were the boom years, still two years before the Great Recession of 2008. But we realized that, in other ways, L.A. was changing. Black neighborhoods just weren't black anymore. About six blocks from his mother's house, we stopped for burgers at a MacDonald's and spotted a HELP WANTED sign. Michael didn't want to ask for an application, but I made him. When he approached the counter and asked for the form, a certain sort of chill passed through the row of Latina women behind the registers. One went and got him the application, and he completed it before we left. But we knew we would not hear anything, and we didn't. We didn't hear anything from anyone else either.

Day after day—under the scorching sun of the worst California heat wave in nearly sixty years—we returned to the cool library and scoured websites for opportunities. We thought maybe it would make sense to focus on large chains— Safeway, Burger King, Best Buy. The thought was that these would have room for advancement inside the organization, if only someone would give Michael, one of so many, a chance. If only he could prove himself. We realized that some of the large companies seemed to have regular days scheduled when they interviewed all comers: Goodwill, Home Depot, Sears. We directed our energies toward them.

One hot day in late July, with temperatures soaring to well over 100, Michael's efforts bore fruit. He was invited in for interviews at Sears and an airport food service company. This was the moment we had been waiting for, but it was, for me, the most terrifying. I don't know if the moment was as fraught for Michael, but I was very anxious about how he could make the case that he ought to be hired—despite having been imprisoned for eleven years since age fifteen for attempted carjacking.

Michael was going to have to tell his story. In full. He had been in prison too long to try to hide that he'd been convicted, not merely of a serious crime but of *the kind of crime* that had sent Los Angeles in the early 1990s into paroxysms of fear. He would have to explain why he believed he was ready to put his life on a new footing. We practiced bits and pieces of his story, but never the whole thing. I never once heard Michael recount his own tale from start to finish, in any version. In hindsight, I think this was because the necessarily abbreviated versions that he was practicing telling his new world would have led me to ask questions. These Michael did not want to deal with.

Only much later would I learn that not even his sister Roslyn, whom we all took to be his truest confidante, was privy to his secrets. Michael had so much constantly to give—stories, reflection, and engagement—that somehow none of us ever noticed just how much he was also withholding, especially by the end. He was a compulsive talker. When he was young, he was a motormouth but with a stammer. We never noticed what the floods of words were obscuring. He could love everybody on the terms on which they needed to be loved; give everybody what they needed to receive, and so, in the end, none of us knew him and, only now, I realize that neither did he know himself.

Michael and I practiced parts of the story. We talked especially about his success as a firefighter and his love of that work. He donned his new khaki trousers and a button-down shirt, and we headed to Hollywood, to Santa Monica and Western, to a Sears. If you folded a map of L.A. in half, north to south, using the 10 Freeway for the crease, Michael's mother's house in South Central and that Sears, now long since shuttered, would have squarely kissed. It felt like the perfect chance.

5.

Upstairs in the Sears personnel department, everything was beige but brightly lit; the baseboards and linoleum floor tiles were well scuffed. The people who greeted us were kind. I sat on one of a row of metal chairs against the wall and waited while Michael, dressed in his khakis, had his interview down the hall in a closed office. I did a lot of waiting during these days. I had a lot of time to think, but I never thought about why I was there. That was never a question. This was my baby cousin, my almost age mate, the youngest of five of us, my brother and I, and our three cousins, staggered like porch steps, each about eighteen months younger than the previous one. We enjoyed being a subset of close cousins within an extended family of cousins who numbered in the dozens. For the five of us, I was the oldest, always the one in charge. I'd been there a few years earlier, too, dragging Michael's older brother, Nicholas, dark-skinned, often somber, through community college. And when I waited, I usually spent my time thinking about my task lists, about what had to be done next. Forty-five long minutes after this particular wait, the door opened and I learned that the managers had offered Michael a job as an inventory clerk.

Relief does not begin to describe it. Time started. That's just what it was like. Now there was a future with stories, possibly even happy endings, suddenly flooding my imagination. Immediately, it seemed okay to think about a day further out than tomorrow. I restrained myself from any actual fantasies, but I now relished the teasing tickle at the edges of my mind from a new dawn. This, I believe, is the most dangerous turn in a journey of this kind, the moment where you begin to hope for real. There is never a reason to let down one's guard. Never. And maintaining such a heightened level of self-discipline, warding off all expectation that something might get easier, is beyond the capacity of most of us. I am speaking for myself here, but I think it was true for Michael, too.

Despite the good news, we stuck to our plan and headed out to LAX so that Michael could have his second interview. We were a team, a duo—Wonder Twin Powers, activate! That we were a team was partly because we were cousins, inextricably close from growing up together, but also because I was the closest family member (in the family-tree sense of "close") with the flexibility and means required to be a steady and consistent presence. There was no one else. Someone's always gotta be the safety net, and it was my at bat.

The drive to LAX is blissful. You can feel the air change as you get closer to the beach. Leaving South Central and riding the bus down Venice Boulevard from just north of the 10, through Mid-City and Culver City, would become one

of Michael's favorite things to do in just a few months' time.
We'd all loved bodysurfing in the frigid Pacific when we
were kids—always best when the surf from some storm at sea
brought in bigger waves. Inevitably, we'd defrost by burying
each other in the hot sand before snacking on Oreos, grapes,
and potato chips, and then throwing Nerf footballs around.
We'd get so hot again that we'd have to plunge back into the
ocean. I think this ride out to LAX was Michael's first beach-
ward trip since he'd come home. Even with the visual field
distortions and fumes of jet-fueled liftoffs, you can still sense
the sea as you get close to the airport, cross the 405, and the
air dampens. This time we drove into the back side of the airport, where the hangars and offices and support services are,
and Michael interviewed for a second job, preparing food for
airplanes at LAX.

He got that one, too. The hiring manager told him, "I want
to hire you. I like your smile." Yes, Michael's beautiful smile.
Always the first thing everyone noticed. Not that they immediately noticed that with his high cheekbones, teak skin, wide
grin, and lithe frame, he was beautiful, which he was; but they
were instantly drawn to him as to the sun. He was a source of
vitality and warmth.

6.

INVESTIGATION, July 2009

The Saturday morning after Michael's body was discovered, and just after Karen herself had gotten the call about Michael's body from the police, a Los Angeles County sheriff's car was parked outside her house. It was still the early dawn. A dread-filled Roslyn, having grabbed whatever sweats and hoodie were to hand and rushed out of her own house at her mother's vague call, spotted the car and knew that her baby brother was dead. Her mother was relieved that she had come. She didn't have any information that she could give the police, but she thought that Roslyn, who was so close to Michael, might provide more help.

My aunt had expected Michael home Thursday night, two days before, and so was consumed with anxiety all day Friday and into the night. Over the course of the week, the normally warm July temperatures had slumped below average. Her dread had only increased alongside the chill. Roslyn, too, had been consumed with worry. On Monday, she dreamed that someone had told her Michael was dead. She woke in tears. When she told Michael about the dream, he said, "My life ain't like that to where I'll be dead."

But he also said, "Sis, if anything happens to me, tell the police it was Bree." Bree was Michael's girlfriend.

Roslyn and Michael spoke by cell phone almost every day. That week, increasingly anxious, Roslyn redoubled her efforts to stay in touch. On Friday, Michael didn't pick up for her all day. When he didn't pick up, she could sometimes tell from the sound of the ring that he was traveling, or had turned his phone off. His phone had rung funny like that on Friday.

Like her mother, Roslyn didn't have much to tell the police, beyond the story about her dream and her brother's warning, but the detectives had things to tell them.

To them Michael was not Michael but "Big Mike." He was someone not to be messed with on the street. This was news, and shocking.

I myself would learn this only much later on. The day before Michael died, evening UK time, while I was conversing with my philosopher husband and catching up on some pleasure reading, I got a rare message from Michael. It would have been Thursday, midmorning, L.A. time, when he'd sent it. Just a few weeks earlier, he'd been at our wedding in New Jersey, where I had an appointment at a distinguished research institute, famous for being Einstein's place of abode. The trip to our wedding was Michael's first airplane flight since his release.

THE AUTHOR AND HER COUSIN, MICHAEL, AT HER WEDDING

That June wedding in New Jersey was my second one. I hadn't invited anyone but my parents and one friend to the first. To my eternal shame, I hadn't even invited my brother. This time I wanted all my family standing by me, joining in the bond I was about to form. Despite having been close to Bob, my first husband, Michael was the usher, greeting every guest at the door with joy.

After that celebratory day, I'd sent Michael a photo of the two of us, me in my splurge Armani dress, he, typically handsome in a beige jacket and crimson shirt. His matching crimson alligator-skin shoes, which made us smile, were, sadly, not visible in the frame.

After he got the photo, he'd written me to say thank you:

7/16/09

MICHAEL ALLEN <MICHAELALLEN4@YAHOO.COM>
6:47 P.M.

Thank you for my picture. I'm sorry to say that I don't check my e mail often and haven't since I printed the plane tickets. I love you so much and I am happy that you are happy and enjoying yourself. I will call you Saturday but I don't know what time is good so be sure to let me know. I love you and I miss you.

> Love Always,
> Michael

These were the kinds of small scraps that we could share about his final twenty-four hours: that on Thursday at 10:47 A.M. he'd used a computer. I am lucky, I suppose, that those words were my final contact.

The police put out a request for help:

Anyone with information about the incident is encouraged to contact Criminal Gang/Homicide Group, 77th Homicide Squad Detectives R. Guzman and K. White at 213-485-1383. During off-hours, calls may be directed to a 24-hour, toll-free number at 1-877-LAPD-24-7 (527-3247). Callers may also text "Crimes" with a cell phone or log on to www.lap donline.org and click on Web tips. When using a cell phone, all messages should begin with "LAPD." Tipsters may remain anonymous.

Beyond this, all we knew was that the police were looking for a woman, and that Bree, Michael's good-looking hairstylist girlfriend, was nowhere to be found. Nor, presumably, was her gold Mercedes.

7.

Michael chose the Sears job. It was obviously the better option—far easier to get to than the job at LAX, and more reliable and promising, too. It was also a bigger operation, so it offered more opportunities generally, social and otherwise.

Having secured a job, our attention turned to school and housing. We had a checklist, a mission, and expected teamwork to get us through. The goal was for Michael to work full-time and to enroll in one of California's famed community colleges. About half a century earlier, these junior colleges had been a remarkable pathway to opportunity, a true engine of mobility for the Golden State. By 2006, they were no longer free, but they were still a good deal.

Now I was in my element. After all, I was the one who knew about schools. Michael's mother Karen hadn't completed college. His brother Nicholas, an on-again, off-again security guard, had tried but not made it through Los Angeles Community College in Culver City. His sister Roslyn had never started. As for me, pretty much my deepest expertise was in going to school. That summer I had reenrolled, only this time with Michael.

Los Angeles Valley College, in Valley Glen, was the obvious target, a decent school with good general education courses and a fire technology program. Its alumni included Tom Selleck and Kevin Spacey, and the subway's Red Line had stops at Santa Monica and Vermont, about a mile from the Sears, and in North Hollywood, not too far from the campus.

During his first year in prison, Michael, a compulsively good and imaginative writer, had completed his GED at lightning speed and over the eleven ensuing years had completed a handful of liberal arts correspondence college courses from the University of Indiana. We reviewed the L.A. Valley College courses with an eye to laying the path toward the school's fire technology program. That was the goal. We battled our way through the thicket of federal financial aid forms, which also required that Michael register for the Selective Service, which he hadn't yet had occasion to do, because of having been in prison. But as we hurdled one after another bureaucratic obstacle, we also found the peaceful quiet of the campus—nearly empty during those dog days of August—to be the balm of Gilead. We found an especially quiet spot, a single maroon picnic table boldly placed amid tumbling boulders and desert plants. Relieved that the July heatwave had broken, the most intense and deadly in over half a century, we sunned ourselves there without talking. After we rested, we would tackle the next event. We visited the tutoring center and library and hungrily collected and studied the various flyers posting internships, jobs, and apartments for rent.

HERE WERE THE GATES of opportunity. In Homer's ancient Greek poem the *Odyssey*, dreams that tell you the truth are said to have come through the gates of horn; the ones that deceive you, through gates of ivory. We believed that the entrance portico to Los Angeles Valley College was the poet's fabled gates of horn. And Michael was poised to pass through.

THE ENTRANCE TO LOS ANGELES VALLEY COMMUNITY COLLEGE—THE POET'S "GATES OF HORN"

8.

The day of Michael's funeral was strenuous. It was a full day of churchgoing and family meals, all on strained emotions.

After his release, Michael had been attending a church we'll call Pillar of Fire, a single-story church with a blaze of lettering to call in wayward souls. Pillar of Fire had also been the family's church years earlier when Michael was arrested and went to prison. His mother, Karen, had since that time fallen out completely with the pastor, Andrew Rinehart, a tall, slender man, his all-gray hairline well receded, who wore spectacles and regal biblical robes of red with gold thread, as he preached under fluorescent lights.

> *See that band all dressed in red;*
> *God's a-going to trouble the water;*
> *Looks like the band that Moses led;*
> *God's a-going to trouble the water.*

Now Karen and Pastor Rinehart were not on speaking terms. She had come to consider her pastor's morality a matter mainly of show. His friends included shady characters, among them one particularly notorious pimp, whose eulogy he had delivered. She had learned from him how to serve him—cleaning the church, running errands, getting the doors to open on time. But she had also learned that she wanted instead to serve God.

For Michael, though, Andrew Rinehart had been a steady, adult presence, and a male one, during a troubled adolescence. After he was released from prison, Michael went back to Pillar of Fire. In the last weeks of his life, during L.A.'s famously misty June days, he spent time at the church, sitting on its rooftop, just being by himself. Since childhood, rooftops had always been the places he sought out to escape his inner conflict.

His mother came only gradually to realize that he never knew himself. He was so good at mirroring what people wanted to see in him that he never had the chance to clarify to himself who he really was. And so, she says, he sought out rooftops to try to get a focus on himself.

> *Temptations, hidden snares, often take us unawares.*
> *And our hearts are made to bleed for a thoughtless word*
>   *or deed.*
> *And we wonder why the test when we try to do our best.*
> *But we'll understand it by and by.*

Pastor Rinehart would have to do the funeral. Michael was his parishioner, after all. But Karen believed that nothing Pastor Rinehart could do would be godly, so she wanted another service at her own church, Bethlehem Temple, at Bethlehem where a child was born. To get in two services for one funeral, we had to start early in the day. And so we did.

Bethlehem Temple mounted a service like those from my childhood when I visited my Baptist grandfather preacher in southern Georgia. Here, too, there were soul-busting songs and unpainted, tee-totaling women; women in hats, with fans, on the verge of fainting. I don't know what I wore, what I looked like, except that it must have been, basically, a "yuppie" look, though in black because it was a funeral. Karen had to be held, and the preacher lifted the roof off. We wept enough to make our own riverside.

> *Oh, we'll wait till Jesus comes*
> *Down by the riverside;*
> *Oh, we'll wait till Jesus comes*
> *Down by the riverside.*

I remember pews wide enough to hold twenty or more, pale blue carpet, and under a very gently sloping roof all was airiness and light.

> *Trials dark on every hand, and we cannot understand.*
> *All the ways that God could lead us to that blessed prom-*
> *   ised land.*
> *But He guides us with His eye, and we'll follow till we die.*
> *For we'll understand it by and by.*

The service was followed by a brief lunch back at Karen's house, and then it was onward to Pillar of Fire. Here the scene

was different. The street had turned out for this service, bringing its jive step. The place was full, but with so many people
we didn't recognize. The detectives were here, too, working.
They hadn't solved the murder yet. They were watching to see
who showed up. Here, on each side of the aisle, the pews held
no more than eight people. Even with its fluorescent lights the
space felt dark under a low, flat ceiling. The wall-to-wall blue
carpet was matched by velour blue upholstery on the chairs
and on the carpeted platform that served as chancel. Self-
involved and self-pitying, Pastor Rinehart used his eulogy to
wrap himself in the accomplishments of the other men in the
chapel. I, dearly beloved, he thundered and I paraphrase, am
the reason that so-and-so sitting just there was a business success, that thus-and-such on the other side of the chapel had
held high office, and yet nobody did any more give credit
where credit was due. Then he descended into an anti-Semitic
rant about money-lenders and lawyers and the difficulty they
brought to those just trying to get by. Between this rant and
the lurking presence of the police, a situation reminiscent of
the opening of *The Godfather*, my British husband of scarcely a
month was slack-jawed.

Where was Michael in all of these remarks?

He was not there. Not in those words, nor, in fact, in his
casket. We'd had a viewing a few days earlier. I'd been set
back, seeing him, his still face so somberly in repose, with a
slightly grayish tinge. There he lay in the satin-lined casket,
in the very suit he'd worn to my wedding a month earlier. For
the first time, I saw how big he looked. At five feet eight he
was two inches shorter than I am, and I had never thought of
him as big. But as I looked at my little cousin's settled face, I

was astonished by his solidity. I had never noticed how much he had bulked up. In the casket, there was no smile. The light was gone and with it, I suppose, the lightness.

Later, much later, writing this, I've had to face the fact that on that day at that viewing I was looking at "Big Mike" lying there, not at little Michael. A poet's line runs, adjusted, through my head:

> *The great grounding*
> *events in your life*
> *. . . the great grounding events that left you so changed*
> *[I] cannot conceive your face without their*
> *happening. . .*

Learning to see when and how Big Mike replaced Michael has been the hardest part of my journey of coming to grasp what happened to my cousin. The old song says, "we'll understand it by and by," and the photographic record does show us when the light went out. We'll get to that eventually, a little further on in the story, but only after we have hit the great grounding events.

At that dismal funeral, so dispiriting, I realized Michael was no longer there; he was not on his rooftop. After the viewing, he was cremated, so there was not even a casket. And Pastor Rinehart's eulogy also obliterated Michael's spirit. Yet the pastor had enough remaining intuition—that something had been left undone—that he invited anyone who wished to come to the dais to testify. My younger brother, Marc, a six-foot-four loose-limbed leader of men, unfolded himself from the pew and showed us all, for the very first time, that he could orate.

"I really loved Michael," he began, and paused, waiting three heart beats.

"Didn't you?"

He painted a picture of the loving, lively, impish Michael he had known. He prayed for his soul. So love rose, in my brother's words and radiant face, and Michael was there after all.

After the service, a woman with small children whom my aunt Karen didn't know came up and tried to press into her hand a wad of money.

"Big Mike was so good to us," she said.

"He always looked after us. He made sure we were okay."

This is how we began to get glimmerings of so much we didn't know.

After the service, we went to Aunt Karen's house for one last homecoming celebration for Michael, gone now for good like so many other millions. Next to that postage stamp of a lawn, we all gathered round folding chairs pulled up to portable tables, laden with fried chicken and sweet tea, to celebrate the baby of the family once more.

We had lost him at fifteen to jail. Then eleven years later he was restored to us. Now at twenty-nine, we had lost him again. We were commemorating, really, what we called not his homecoming but his homegoing, how he'd gotten over to the promised land.

> *How I got over,*
> *How I got over, my Lord*
> *And my soul looked back and wondered*
> *How I got over, my Lord?*

Oh, Jordan's river is so chilly and cold
It will chill your body but not your soul
And my soul looked back and wondered
How I got over, my Lord.

The adults were tired and slack. My first and second husbands had a chance to have their first extended conversation. Lunch and talk and afternoon went long enough that they made their peace with one another and, by and by, the kids fifteen and under, those too young to remember the preincarceration Michael, were running races in the narrow street between the parked cars, with two uncles marking the finish line and calling out the winner. Michael's niece was the fastest, a future champion. We all stood round to watch and took some pleasure in it.

"She's fast like you were," her dad, Michael's brother, my cousin Nicholas, said to me.

9.

APARTMENT, August 2006

In the weeks after Michael's release, he and I worked together, constantly, assembling the pieces of a possible life, as if doing a jigsaw puzzle. First we laid the job piece in. Then the piece with the school shape. If this new beginning was going to work, everything would have to nestle just so.

We both knew that. We both knew that the next necessary piece was a place to live. It was the chance for him to be an adult on his own, not to live with his mother. I also knew that it needed to be close to school or work. I was clear-eyed that the whole arrangement would take only if the three core pieces—home, work, school—joined perfectly, but the place needed to be cheap enough that Michael could manage it on his scant Sears wages. Each of us scoured the listings. Together, we drove by the addresses, made calls and appointments, and began to sort through our options.

And then we found the perfect place. On Ethel Avenue in Valley Glen, a few blocks north of the community college, someone was advertising a studio apartment in a converted garage behind a modest home. We phoned—I don't remember which of us placed the call—and the studio was still available. They were prepared to show it to us. Michael practiced telling his story.

The home was impeccable, a modest white bungalow, typical of a certain vintage of Los Angeles, with a mid-torso-high white iron fence surrounding the house, broken up at each twenty feet by a whitewashed stucco column. White concrete had supplanted the front lawn so there was enough room to park two vehicles. Alongside the fence stood some small, neatly tended shrubs and rose bushes spraying white roses.

I went up to the house by myself. Two women met me at the door, a mother most likely in her sixties, and her daughter, in her thirties or forties. They were Latinas, or maybe Middle Eastern. For all of the outdoor brightness of the white house on its white concrete yard and pearly white roses, the inside was dark and cramped, though neat as a pin. Dressed in linen trousers with a black t-shirt and comfy sandals, I introduced myself.

I was a professor, I told them, and I was helping my cousin who had recently been released from prison. He had just enrolled at Los Angeles Valley College and gotten a job at Sears. I would be paying his deposit and guaranteeing his rent. He'd gone to prison as a young person and this was his second chance. He was ready for it. Were they willing to meet him and to let him tell his story?

They agreed, and this time I sat outside while Michael spoke to his prospective landlords. He could charm anyone with his bouncing gait and toothy, flashing grin. Finally, the three emerged, now with smiles on all their faces, and they took us around to the back to see the studio. It was whitewashed just as cleanly as the house. It had a hotplate, and an electric heater. Probably it wasn't insulated. But it was clean and peaceful. Had it been for me, I could have imagined being comfortable there. And it was walking distance from the school.

Michael said, yes, he wanted it. We all shook hands in the gaze of the late afternoon sun. Since the day was nearly over, I agreed to bring a cashier's check the following day. As we drove back to South Central, my mood was all melody. I imagined Michael felt the same. When those two women looked at us and said, yes, we could rent the studio, I experienced their act of trust and generosity as a gift beyond comprehension. I experience it equally so to this day.

So we had done it.

Little more than a month out and here was Michael, now with a driver's license, a bank account, a library card, and a job. He was enrolled in college, with an affordable, convenient, clean, safe, and comfortable place to live. These were the concrete, material, nonillusory basics, a starter set for a life. We had established the realistic possibility of a future, even if Michael had had to move back to the asphalt jungle that is Los Angeles instead of going straight to a fire camp. We had begun a passage through the gates of horn, I was sure of it.

In my white BMW, I dropped him off in South Central and headed back to Hollywood, expecting to sleep soundly for the first time in a spell. But then Michael called. He wasn't sure he should take the apartment. I felt a stone drop from a great height to the bottom of a well.

Why not, I asked?

He just wasn't sure it felt right.

Didn't feel right, I asked?

He couldn't explain, he said. He just didn't feel quite right about it.

I told him to sleep on it. We'd talk in the morning, I said.

Morning came, as it must, and I called Michael. He wanted the apartment, he said. Relieved, I headed off to do the necessary banking, and Michael headed off under yet another cloudless sky to his job at Sears. He called me at midday. Had I taken the check over yet, he wanted to know? I said I had not, because I had imagined picking him up after work so that we could do it together. He had, he said, changed his mind yet again.

He didn't think he wanted the apartment after all.

"What?" I expostulated.

I was shocked. I peppered him with questions.

"What do you mean you don't want the apartment? Michael, what on earth are you talking about?"

Michael responded that he wasn't sure what it would be like if his associates came by.

From a remove, I recall that the word surprised me, but I didn't ask him what he meant by "associates." The purpose of the word, somehow, was to insist on his privacy, and it brought me up sharp. I didn't understand all of that then. I just paused, sucked in my surprise, didn't ask questions. I told him to go ahead and think about it some more. Disagreement was rare for us.

He called me a few hours later. He said he would take the apartment and that I should pick him up after work.

But then, just before we were to meet, he called again. "I've made up mind," he said. "I don't want the apartment."

I was stunned. I could not imagine any possible grounds

for walking away from a viable set of arrangements. And we had, I thought, developed all the details of the plan together, based on his desires and my advice. Michael had not given me any glimmer of a suggestion that he had hopes or fears that might derail the plans we were developing. Perhaps I wasn't listening well enough, but I don't think that's it. I think he had finely honed his skills at seeming to be wholly present while also holding significant parts of himself out of view.

I'm sure we exchanged some sharp words. I must have asked some angry questions. But I don't remember any of that last conversation other than his decisiveness.

What was his plan instead? I must have asked at least that much. His plan was to live with his mother and to ride the bus from there to Sears and from there to Los Angeles Valley Community College. This was a triangle of 8.6 x 9.8 x 21.9 miles. For someone who didn't have a car. Through the worst of Los Angeles traffic.

It was clear, though, that there was nothing I could do. It was by now well into August. School would start soon. I would have incoming students to welcome, new faculty to orient, and budgets to plan. I bought him more khakis and button-down shirts, spent as much time with him as I could, and headed back to Chicago when I had to.

Over the course of that summer, though, I had decided to leave my job as dean. I would take up a less time-intensive research position in New Jersey. When I got back, the first task on my checklist was to tell the university's provost and then the president.

10.

HITTING BOTTOM,
November 2006

Because he had us—his family, his clan—I believed Michael could defy the pattern of parolees. College was the first element to fall out of the plan. The commute was, not surprisingly, just too much. Michael may not have made it through even two weeks of classes. The job lasted until November, and then I got a nearly hysterical call. Michael was drowning. He couldn't do it, he said. He wasn't going to make it. When I had left L.A., with plans to return over the winter break, I had promised him that if, in the meanwhile, he ever called and said he needed me, I would be there. Receiving his call, I went straight to O'Hare. I flew across the country west of the Mississippi in a cold panic, trying to forestall speculation about what I might find. Arriving just in time to take him to dinner, I found Michael teary and despondent. With only twenty-four hours to spend in Los Angeles, I tried to lift him off the bottom.

His account of what had happened was that one day after work some of his Latino coworkers had called him nigger. He fought them in the parking lot, and walked away from the job, never to return. He never told his bosses or coworkers that he was quitting. He just didn't go back.

So now he was back to square one, or less than that, since now he'd proven himself unreliable to an employer. He was mostly spending his time at home, in the house, playing Football and Basketball Workout video games with Joshua and Josh's little brother.

This is, in fact, the best recipe for safety in rough neighborhoods: stay inside at all times with young kids for companions.

Sometimes, though, craving adult company, Michael would hang out at the little informal restaurant around the corner from his mother's house.

Now he didn't see a future. Didn't know what steps to take next. The world hadn't yielded up the fruits he'd fantasized at the end of the summer.

Nor was it supplying those I had dreamed of.

I didn't have much to offer. I tried mainly to listen. I could promise to get him into an apartment, if he could get another job. But I wasn't in a position now to stay in Los Angeles and help him pursue new job possibilities. I had too many obligations in Chicago. November was tenure review time, with mounds of scholarly papers to read and discuss in an unending cycle of meetings that the dean, in particular, is not supposed to miss. If anything, the very definition of being a dean is to be at those tenure review meetings. My own professional reputation was at stake. Michael would have to make the next push for himself. I would be back in a few weeks for the Christmas holidays and would be able to spend more time with him then.

So I did keep my promise and come when he called, but I suppose in the end I wasn't there for him as I had promised.

Just before the winter break, the university made the public announcement of my decision to step down at the end of the academic year. Bob and I flew out to L.A., both feeling newly unburdened, happy to escape Chicago's precipitous chill, and looking forward to winter oranges and nuts. Shortly after we arrived in L.A., I got a good-news call from Michael. He'd found an apartment. He was ready to put the deposit down. Could I come and see it? Michael and I visited the fourth-floor unit, in a vintage 1920s building with Craftsman-style features, overlooking the 101 Freeway, just off of Fountain. It was big and spacious, with gleaming wood floors, and Michael began describing to me how he and his girlfriend Bree wanted to move in.

I was taken aback. I had had no idea he was seeing someone, let alone making plans to move in together. I imagine that my face must have conveyed surprise, although I think I tried not to react too strongly. Learning how to suppress visible emotion is an occupational hazard of deaning. What I wanted to know, I said, was what the job situation was. Had he lined up a new job? What did Bree do? Did she have a job? Our voices were echoey in the empty apartment, Michael leaning against a windowsill with the sky and freeway backdrop.

This was the one and only time in my life when my interaction with my cousin had an edge. There was somehow something shamefaced in him as he answered. No, he didn't have a job. Bree was into hairstyling but, no, she didn't have one either. What exactly were they thinking, I found myself asking? He didn't have much of an answer and plainly the plan involved some degree of taking advantage of me.

In that moment, I encountered a different Michael from the one I knew. I saw something calculating, which I had never seen and would never see again. I didn't ask to talk to Bree. All I was able to say was that, no, I couldn't possibly pay the deposit plus some number of months' rent plus cosign for an apartment when neither of them had jobs.

Michael's face tensed.

He said he understood.

And that was the end.

I had believed that I could help. I had hoped we were entering the gate of horn, the passage of true dreams. Now, and only now, I realized that my dream of standing my baby cousin up on his own two feet was a fantasy. It had always had, perhaps, too much of me in it. From this point on, Michael ceased confiding in me. Our phone conversations never crawled below the surface. I no longer knew a way of helping. I couldn't have, really, because I no longer knew what was going on.

I later learned that in the following months Michael had started working as a plumber's apprentice for a friend of his mother's. He had earned several vocational certificates while in prison. And he spent time with Bree. We would learn her possessiveness was violent, yet Michael spent increasing amounts of time with her. According to Karen, Bree cut him three times between December and May, and each time Michael tried to pass the cuts off as the result of someone attempting to rob him.

His mother would, almost kiddingly, tell him, "Michael, I really have to get some life insurance on you," but he did not say no.

Not quite a year after his release, in May or June 2007, Michael got into a fight with one of Bree's lovers. He suspected Bree of cheating and thought that if he could catch her and confront her, he would have a way out of the relationship. Late one night, he sneaked up under her window to catch them.

Michael related the story in a letter: "I wish every day that I would've stayed in bed. But how could I when my stomach was telling me that she was cheating? I figured if I catch her cheating, then I could resolve the relationship right there and then. I didn't have the will to say it was over, but surely if I caught her in the act cheating then it would make ending it more simple. I was wrong, Danielle, dead wrong. Needless to say me and the guy had an altercation. He called the police and now I'm here."

Michael went straight from the altercation to prison for a parole violation. This pushed back the date of his sentence completion by a full year, from June 2008 to June 2009. I wish I could describe how I felt when I got this news, but I just can't.

It was such a catastrophic defeat that after Michael's death, my memory obliterated all traces of his return to prison. I guess I sent him a few packages and must have written a couple of letters because I have his. But I was in a bad state before the news came—my marriage to Bob was coming apart. The intersecting professional and personal demands on each of us were beyond what we could handle together. And I simply have no memory of Michael's second phase in prison, perhaps because of the torturous fighting as we moved toward separation, perhaps because of the magnitude of the defeat.

For years after Michael died, I told people that my cousin went to prison when he was fifteen, got out when he was twenty-six, and died one year later. A permanent amnesia seems to have erased the time from his second trip to prison to the end of his life. It was only when I came across an August 2007 email from Karen with a prison address for Michael that I realized— and it wouldn't be correct to say "remembered"—that he'd gone back. There is a seed of truth in this trick of my memory. Other than just superficially, I was not there for Michael's last two years, one back in prison and that final year, still on parole, until, in his final three weeks alive, he was, officially at least, free at last. The disappearance of this stretch of time and what I presume was also my disappearance on Michael are probably the most painful and shameful things I have to admit.

Now able to correct the distortions brought on by my shame, though, I can confirm that the barebones facts of my cousin's biography are these. He was born on November 30, 1979, when Barbara Streisand's "No More Tears" was the country's number-one song. On September 18, 1995, at fifteen, two weeks before O. J. Simpson was acquitted for the murder of his wife, Michael was arrested for the first time for an attempted carjacking. On June 10, 1996, five days after the first birthday of the niece who, like me, would grow up to be a track star, he was sentenced to twelve years and eight months in prison. In November 1996, on his seventeenth birthday, he was transferred to adult prison. He got out of prison in June of 2006 when he was twenty-six, just before the Great North American Heatwave killed over 200 people. He went back in in June of 2007 when he was twenty-seven, got out again in August of 2008 when he was twenty-eight, and was finally clear of all parole in June 2009. Less than a month later on July 18, 2009, at the age of twenty-nine, he died.

One of so many millions gone.

II.

THE END,
August 2008–July 2009

The light went out of Michael's eyes during his second stint in prison. Inmates get to take formal pictures, rather like the annual pictures kids take in school. They also get to take pictures with their visitors.

We have a whole series of pictures of Michael growing up in prison. I see the Michael I always knew in all of them up until the last image, which was snapped during his second imprisonment.

In those early pictures, it's his smile, easy and giving; partly, it's also a certain openness in his eyes. These qualities make him recognizable, at least to me, in all the earlier photos. Both those things are gone in the last picture.

The smile and the eyes withhold.

When Michael finally did get out the second time, during those final heady weeks of Barack Obama's history-shattering first presidential campaign and just weeks before the market crash that would consume a distant world of elites, he returned

MICHAEL ALLEN, IN CENTRAL
JUVENILE, WITH MOTHER,
KAREN ALLEN, AUTUMN 1995

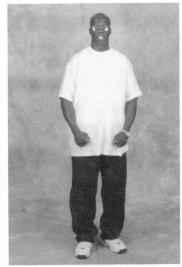

MICHAEL ALLEN IN CALIFORNIA
REHABILITATION CENTER—
NORCO, DATE UNCERTAIN

MICHAEL ALLEN IN CALIFORNIA
REHABILATATION CENTER—
NORCO, DATE UNCERTAIN

MICHAEL AND KAREN ALLEN,
VISITING DAY IN CALIFORNIA
REHABILITATION CENTER—
NORCO, 2004

MICHAEL ALLEN,
DURING SECOND PHASE
IN PRISON, 2007-2008

to what we hoped would be the comfort of his mother's house. In a matter of weeks, though, she would need heart surgery, and this would consume them both. For several months, while the world seemed to hang from a precipice, Karen's ever-devoted son nursed her back to health, but as the fall progressed, he spent less and less time with her. He would still come round—orderly style—to check that she had what she needed, that she had taken her medications, and that she was comfortable. But he had begun to live with Bree.

In the months before Michael's parole violation, Karen and Bree had developed a strong mutual dislike, fighting a subterranean battle. Now, with Michael out again, Bree sought a formal treaty. She called Karen to say that Michael would be living with her and that she didn't want conflict.

This was understandably hard for Karen. The relationship

between the two ex-convicts was violent. Bree, too, had been in prison, for attempted murder, as Karen understood it, and Karen's protective motherly instincts were on red alert. She never saw her son get physical with anyone except once when she saw Michael fight with Bree on her tidy front lawn. Bree had been going down the street breaking the windows on people's cars and throwing things at the walls of Karen's house. Michael had gone outside to warn her never to come round again. The two started to fight. Through a window, Karen saw Michael knock Bree out. Startled, she rushed out to bring a halt to things.

The trouble was hardly confined to this one altercation. The only time Karen or Roslyn ever saw Michael drunk was during this period after the second time he got out. He had recently reconnected with Devonn, the friend who thirteen years earlier had been his partner in the attempted carjacking. Michael came home with him one night from a party where people had been serving him Pink Panties (ice cream mixed with vodka, pink lemonade, and ice, then put in a blender to make it like a shake). They're also called "Creepers" because the alcohol sneaks up on you. Weeping, Michael could barely stand and was screaming, crying hysterically first to his mother, and then to Pastor Rinehart on the phone, that he wanted nothing more than to get away from Bree but also couldn't stay away. The words of another ancient poet, Catullus this time, might have been his own: "I hate and I love. Why I do so, perhaps you ask? I know not, but I feel it, and I am in torment."

In October, Roslyn helped him get a job at a television studio where she worked nights transcribing the recordings of sitcoms that had been taped during the day. Imagine a room full of people clacking out our prefab dreams. Michael began sleeping with a friend of his sister's who worked there. When Bree found out, she began harassing her rival with obsessive phone calls that escalated into threats. In November, just as Barack Obama broke the patterns of American history, Michael quit the job.

That same month, Michael, for the first time, broke a promise to his sister, or seemed to have done so. She had communicated with him by text, asking him to help her move. He had promised to be there, but he never showed. With Michael, this sort of unreliability had been unheard of. Eventually, Roslyn learned that he had never gotten her messages. Bree was stealing his phone and responding to his texts, pretending to be Michael, to cut him off from his other worlds—his family, his other romantic relationships.

Every six months, Michael went to get his blood checked. He had at some point become HIV positive. Karen and I didn't know about this. Only Roslyn knew. She believes he told the four women he slept with of this fact. After his death, his mother put out word that she was ready to acknowledge any children he may have had and contribute to their support, but no one came forward to claim such a relationship. This is all we know about the tangled weave of his relationships.

By December, when much of the rest of the country was hoping that Barack Obama would be able to steer the country away from the cliff, Michael's world fully contracted. It was then, living at Bree's house, that he became Big Mike, driving her Mercedes or her second set of wheels, a green Subaru truck. That winter, he revealed to Roslyn a gun, hidden wrapped in a towel, in the Mercedes. By spring, he was running drugs, including at least one trip to Texas. Records reveal that on May 15, 2009, he got a speeding ticket in border country—Arizona, Pima County. Later, the detectives investigating his murder found marijuana and PCP in his room. It's still so hard for me to put the pieces together, but during this time Bree and Michael also appear to have attempted to rob a gas station. Nor was that the whole of the trouble. Something else, unnameable, seems also to have happened in that period.

Bree and Michael had their big fight on Karen's front lawn, the one where he knocked her out, that same May. Maybe the argument had something to do with the trip through Pima County. It's impossible to say. That night when Bree began smashing car windows, Karen wanted to call the police, but Michael urged her not to, saying, that if the police came they would put him away for a very, very long time because "he had hurt two people real bad." Then, as Michael and Bree thrashed outside, Karen heard Bree threatening to call the police on Michael. Michael responded that since she had been there too, she would just get herself in trouble if she did.

Karen also heard Michael say, "Go on, then. Tell your cousin to call a hit on me," the most glaring piece of evidence that he was now fully ensconced in a world of hit men, where people kill on orders.

Starting from that night, Karen added to her prayers, her constant talks with God, the hope that the Lord would liberate Michael from his misery. "I just wanted Michael out of his conflict," she recalls. Later, for all the pain of losing her beautiful baby boy, Karen also found some kind of peace in it. Death, she believes, had become his only possible release.

The theologian Augustine captured her experience, I think,

more than a millennium ago. "It is true, then, that the life of mortals is afflicted, sometimes more gently, sometimes more harshly, by the death of those most dear to us. And yet we should prefer to hear, or even to witness, the death of those we love, than to become aware that they have died in their very soul. The earth is full of this vast mass of evils; that is why we find in Scripture, 'Is man's life on earth anything but temptation?' And why the Lord himself says, 'Alas for the world, because of these obstacles.'"

While I was consumed by travel and lecturing, and a new job in New Jersey, Karen and Roslyn were the only people by Michael's side, intuiting just how bad things had gotten. Karen's prayers for a release for her son acknowledged a truth. Roslyn's final Monday dream that someone came to tell her Michael had died also emerged from that unguarded quadrant of her soul that already understood the trajectory of her brother's life. Yet mother and daughter tended to these chilling intuitions separately.

Even with one another, they did not share the small, still voices that spoke from their hearts. Those of us who were further away had no idea. Even when we came together, we could not see. We could not apprehend the demons chasing Michael as he greeted our wedding guests at the door to the chapel.

Just shy of a month past that glorious champagne-filled June wedding day, when Jim and I set out on a new life together, the police picked up Bree for petty theft and a prior record. Two weeks later, although she was already in prison, they issued an arrest warrant for her for Michael's killing and charged her with murder with malice aforethought. She had shot Michael in her kitchen.

There had been one witness. A middle school age boy. He'd heard, not seen, the events. But there were voices, a hit, and gun shots. With the help of relatives, Bree cleaned Michael up nicely, even prettifying him. She then bundled him in a blanket, put him in his little hatchback, and drove him to the street-corner where he was found. Three accessories—all members of Bree's family—were also charged.

Bree pled not guilty.

To prove its case, the prosecution prepared, among other things, to introduce a pattern of acts of violence perpetrated by Bree. As the transcript of the proceedings reports:

> People intend to introduce evidence of a 2003 assault with a firearm by Ms Brent. In that case, Ms Brent allegedly shot at a man who was at a bus stop with her. The man was laughing and mocking her because he believed she was a man. The people allege that that uncharged crime is material to the issue of motive in this case.

The public defender prepared a defense. Again, the record reports:

> Ms. Brent was in a dating relationship with the deceased for many years, prior to this incident. The two had a turbulent relationship in which Mr. Allen would hurt, threaten, assault and stalk Ms. Brent. The relationship unfortunately came to an end on the date of this incident. This case is in no way similar or related to the facts in the prior bad act and therefore that act is irrelevant

and immaterial to the facts necessary to prove motive in this case.

A year and a half into the case, with a jury empaneled, Bree took a deal and pled *nolo contendere* ("no contest") to voluntary manslaughter. Under the name Isaiah Brent, she was sentenced to twenty-two years of incarceration, but, this time, since she'd by now undergone gender reassignment surgery, Bree was sent to a women's prison.

Michael and Bree had first met when they were both inmates at the Correctional Rehabilitation Center–Norco, a men's prison, where they had become lovers. A summer baby, Bree was little over two years older than Michael. She was just his height and just his weight. As Karen understood it, Bree was in prison for attempting to kill a boyfriend. As far as the public record reveals, she'd been convicted as Isaiah for assault with a firearm and for threatening injury with the potential to result in death. When she entered Michael's prison at twenty-five, she was a cross-dressing transgender woman still early in the process of transitioning. After she got out, and before Michael came home, she had gender reassignment surgery.

When that gold Mercedes cruised Michael's homecoming back in 2006, it was Bree in her chariot coming for to carry Michael home. We all had thought the relationship ended when Bree left prison a year ahead of Michael, and we believed that Michael's home was with us. What Michael himself thought or wanted that homecoming day, I will never know.

He hadn't invited Bree to the picnic. Yet she came and would stay.

When Michael contemplated renting that tidy little studio apartment on Ethel Avenue, with its white fence and pearly roses, it was voluptuous Bree in her tight clothes and gold Mercedes whom he was visualizing having to introduce to those kindly landladies. How would it have gone if he had taken this "associate" home with him?

When he spent that twenty-four hours dithering over whether to rent the Ethel Avenue apartment, his real question was whether to repudiate the first and only love of his life.

Would he choose Bree?

He did.

And as the poet says, his "arrow flew, as if of itself," from his bow.

Michael had made his life's defining choice.

INFERNO

"Rehabilitation is pretty much out of favor as a concept for juvenile offenders. Now the theory is that they'll learn if you lock them up for long enough. There are obvious problems with that. The criminal justice system has no resources to rehabilitate anyone. But all the existing theories have flaws. When it comes to juvenile crime, frankly nobody in the country and nobody in the world has the answer."

—**AN EXPERT**, quoted in the *Los Angeles Times*, September 6, 1995, "New Wave of Mayhem; Juveniles Are Increasingly Committing Violent Crimes—and Experts Don't Know Why or How Best to Stop Them"

12.

CRIME AND PUNISHMENT

Where were you when you were fifteen? Close your eyes and try to recall. I lived in a bedroom with a brass bed, with a blue-and-white-striped Laura Ashley comforter. There were matching valences on my windows, and I had a wooden rolltop desk, with a drawer that locked and held my secrets, including dirty letters that I couldn't at the time translate from a German boy who'd been the object of a minor summer music camp romance. I was awkward and insecure, confused about how to find my place in life. Often I was lonely. All of this was true despite the fact that I was hurtling into my junior year of high school as captain of my varsity track team.

I was younger than most of my classmates at Claremont High School, and my friends all had their driver's licenses by the start of our junior year. I was not, however, allowed to ride in their cars. The only time I ever got grounded in high school was when my librarian mother caught me sneaking a ride with a friend to get to my French class at the local college. I grew up in a college town, a faculty brat, where everyone knew my mom and dad. My parents had made a critical decision early in the lives of my younger brother Marc and me that, regardless of what career opportunities came my father's way, they would not move until we had graduated from high school. I grew up in one place, where everyone knew me. I couldn't even get away with sneaking to my college courses.

Which of us does *not* remember what life was like at fifteen? The torments of adolescence leave indelible marks.

Eight years after I got grounded for sneaking to class in that friend's car, my fifteen-year-old cousin, Michael Alexander Allen, who also didn't yet have a driver's license, was arrested, for the first time, for an attempted carjacking. A few months later, after he turned sixteen, he sat in Torrance, California, in court, the standard kind with the swinging gates just inside the doors of the courtroom, hands cuffed there and in an orange suit, in December 1995 and January 1996, as a judge determined that he would be charged as an adult.

When he was arrested the previous September, he had been living with Karen, and Roslyn, then seventeen, in their one-bedroom apartment on Imperial Highway in Los Angeles. Teenagers Michael and Roslyn slept in twin beds in the bedroom, only a dresser wedged between them. Karen took the daybed in the living room. I was far away, pursuing graduate school in England, studying crime and punishment in ancient Athens. I had gravitated toward the subject upon being struck by the remarkable fact that a sophisticated, democratic society had existed that made next to no use of imprisonment.

Although visits with Michael and his family had occurred frequently in my childhood, I had seen them mainly over holidays for the previous few years. Along the banks of the faraway river Cam, I shared tentative efforts at poems with friends, debated ancient Athenian politics, and, in June 1994, reeled from O. J. Simpson's desperate attempt at escape and his arrest for murder. My own first professional ambition had been to be a running back. I'm not kidding when I say that Simpson was my inspiration. When the news of Michael's arrest came in September 1995, it was just as stupefying.

Four and a half months after Michael's last night at home, on February 5, 1996, he sat again in court, in yet another orange suit and handcuffs, as the judge told him to choose whether to stand trial and face a possible conviction of twenty-five years to life or to plead guilty and take a reduced sentence. The judge didn't say how much the sentence would be reduced, but he did say, "Please take the plea."

Michael could not choose. Now sixteen, he asked his mother to decide. Karen remembers going outside the courtroom and praying and praying, and then some. "God told me," she says, "that he would only get seven years, versus risking a trial of twenty-five years to life. I made the decision."

So Michael pled guilty in February 1996. Sentencing then took four months. Finally, in June, he received a sentence of sixteen years and six months, with forty-six months to run concurrently. This worked out to twelve years and eight months of actual prison or supervised release, starting from his September arrest. In December the Department of Corrections sought a clarification about his sentence, which resulted in his "earliest possible release date" being set for June 29, 2006. His sentence would be complete on June 29, 2008, barring any changes. In the end, his parole violation had the consequence of pushing that final date back to June 2009. According to Karen, the only time Michael cried in court was when he got sentenced.

When you're sixteen, the farthest back you can remember is only about thirteen years, to the age of three. That's the whole of your life. This means that Michael's sentence was equivalent, in psychological terms, to the whole of his life. Imagine hearing those words, words that mean, "For as many years as you have known and roamed this earth, for so long shall you live enclosed and constrained." To quote Atul Gawande, the doctor and writer, time horizons measured in decades "might as well be infinity to human beings." It must be especially so for the young. Michael's sentence, in other words, stretched to the horizon of what was then for him his known world or the limit of knowable time. In the here and now, he had been given the strange privilege of access to an earthly simulation of eternal damnation, of registering in his sensorium the yawning chasm of infinite punishment.

Recalculations are easy enough. Imagine that you are twenty and someone tells you that you will spend the next sixteen years in one place, plus another four under close surveillance. Or perhaps you are thirty and it will be the next twenty-four years, plus another six under surveillance. Or you are forty and it will be the next thirty-two years, plus another eight in purgatory. The mind cannot fasten onto this sort of temporality, time that extends across all the time that we have already known. We are unable to give these allocations of time concrete meaning in relation to our own lives. The imagination wanders into white space. For inmates with long sentences, time in prison is a time without "milestones," "dead time," "an expanding distance from home," a "gaping abyss," according to researchers. For as creative a young man as Michael, it was, he wrote, "a mountain of time" to climb.

Michael told me once, late in his imprisonment, that he was incredibly grateful to my classy, successful father, Uncle William as he called him, for having constantly had the radio in our house tuned to a classical music station. Michael had spent a lot of time with us in his young childhood, and in his middle school years his family had lived for a stretch in our small college town. And he was right. From the time I came home from school, until I went to bed, the radio in the living room would be playing a public station cycling between news and classical music. Or if we went to ask my father a question as he worked enveloped by plumes of pipe smoke, ensconced in heaps of paper in a book-filled study in a converted garage behind our house, the moment you opened the thin wood door, orchestral harmonies perfumed with the tweedy, comforting smell of tobacco rolled over you.

Michael had discovered that one of the best ways to get through the endless stretches of time in prison was to isolate himself in his bunk and to listen on his radio to classical music. This was not something he did with other inmates; it was a private activity, a choice that to some extent set him apart, just as my father's conservative cultural tastes set him apart within his family.

Although I'd had ten years of classical piano lessons, Michael's remark about his gratitude for classical music in prison finally brought home to me the intrinsic value of symphonic music. Such musical forms sculpt time and render it in sonic form. They convert time's passage, as we sojourners pass through our own earthly prison, into a realm of interest and beauty. In this regard—and I know I am being an apostate—an hour-long symphony or, yes, a three-hour opera have much more to give human beings than the conventional three-minute pop song.

Consider this: thirteen years in prison is equivalent to listening to 37,960 three-hour operas or 2,227,600 pop songs. Or cut those numbers in half for sleeping. Michael got very good at sleeping. A sentence of twelve years and eight months, eight months already served and credited for good behavior, ten more years in prison, and two on parole before freedom—Michael's sentence was long enough for an astonishing musical education, whatever genre he might have chosen.

So what had Michael done to deserve this?

On, September 17, 1995, a cool and foggy Sunday morning, Larry Smith, a forty-four-year-old man, was buffing the dashboard of his blue 1986 Cadillac two-door Coupe de Ville in the alley behind his Rosecrans Avenue apartment, just west of the Normandie Casino. The street was lined, as it is today, with drab, 1960s two-story walk-up stucco apartment buildings, with uncovered staircases leading down from entrances, all on the backside of the building, to carports, "sheltered parking," below. Architects call such buildings "dingbats." Nowadays the atmosphere can be pretty rough. People stare down suspiciously from their landings if you drive by too slowly.

On that distant Sunday, Smith was buffing his car, alongside one stretch of carports, when Michael suddenly appeared holding a chrome .380-caliber gun, a Lorcin 380, a cheap gun given to malfunction. Michael's partner, Devonn, somewhere nearby, was on lookout or something of the sort, but not visible to Smith as he worked in his car. Michael appeared and, as Smith reported to police, said, "Don't move; give me your watch." Smith handed it over.

Then Michael asked for his wallet. When he found it empty, he tossed it back into the car. Then, according to Smith, Michael "tapped Smith's left knee with the gun and said he was going to take the car." According to Smith, Michael kept the gun pointing at the ground, and so Smith, a "lanky" man according to the report, who was two inches shorter than Michael but weighed the same as the fifteen-year-old, lunged for the weapon. They wrestled. Michael punched him. Smith gained control of the gun and shot Michael through the neck. Michael fell to the ground, and thus ended his attempted carjacking.

Smith hollered out to his wife to call 911, and Devonn hightailed it out of there. His house was about a dozen blocks away. Michael lay on the ground bleeding. Smith carefully placed the gun on the ground at some distance from Michael and waited for the police to arrive. When they came, they collected all the evidence and sought witnesses. No one had been outside, but people were at home. No one had anything to say. The Gardena paramedics arrived and transported Michael to Harbor-UCLA hospital, where he was treated for the "through and through" bullet wound that had narrowly missed his spine.

A police officer accompanied Michael in the ambulance and reported that "during transport, Allen made spontaneous statement that he was robbing a man when he got shot." At the hospital, Michael was read his Miranda rights and additional juvenile admonishments in the presence of a second officer. The police report also records that "Allen stated he understood his rights, waived his rights, and made the following statement: "that he had not been home all week, and that he saw the man cleaning his car, and that he decided to rob him." Michael claimed that he had found the pistol about two and a half weeks earlier but provided two different stories about where he found it, saying once that he'd found it in the alley by a McDonald's near his mother's house and once that he'd found it on a walkway at the Rosecrans apartments. He also confessed that he had robbed three people during the previous two days on the same block of Rosecrans, and that he had robbed someone a week earlier, about ten blocks away. The police had no reports of robberies for two of his four confessions, but for the two that had been reported, Michael had taken $20 from one victim and $2 from another. In other words, on his way to the hospital, and upon admission, without adults present other than the officers, Michael, lying there wounded, talked up a blue streak.

Karen sped toward the hospital. She didn't have a phone, and, to the best of our knowledge, the police hadn't made an attempt to contact her. Instead, she was alerted to events by Devonn's sister. As Karen was getting ready for church at Pillar of Fire that Sunday morning, there was a knock on the door. Devonn's sister had been dispatched to tell Karen that Michael had been shot. Karen dropped Roslyn off at church and raced to the hospital. By the time she got there, Michael had already wrapped up his confession. The only thing he didn't mention to the police was Devonn's involvement. Devonn was, in fact, a couple of years older than Michael; the story has always been that the whole thing, and the gun, too, were Devonn's. I have no way of knowing if that's true.

I didn't learn all these details about Michael's crime until much later. All I learned at the time was that he had been arrested for an attempted carjacking. The news caused shock and made my brain race in endless loops.

"How could it be? How could it be? How could it be?"

Up until then, Michael did not have a criminal record.

That day he gained one with a vengeance. The reporting officer checked off physical features from a list of possibilities: "hair length: short; hair type: wiry; hair style: afro-natural; complexion: medium; facial hair: clean shaven; facial shape: high cheekboned; teeth: other." A description of his teeth as "straight" was then written in alongside the line for "other." The form did not anticipate such teeth, only chipped, crooked, false, jeweled, and studded ones.

For the watch and wallet, Michael was charged with robbery, not attempted robbery. For the car, he was charged with attempted carjacking. Both charges were "enhanced" because of the use of the gun. Then he was also charged with the two robberies on the same block from the previous day. Four felonies. This also meant four strikes, two from one incident, and all in one week. This turned out to equal one chance.

Eighteen months earlier, as it so happened, in March of 1994, California's Three Strikes and You're Out Law, the nation's first, had gone into effect. Once you were convicted of your third felony, it was twenty-five years to life, or a plea deal. If he chose to pursue a jury trial, Michael was told by the judge, a conviction on these four charges would, in one fell swoop, trigger the Three Strikes law and bring twenty-five years to life.

In October of 1994, the *Los Angeles Times* ran the first in a series of articles on the new Three Strikes law. The title was

"Six Months of 'Three Strikes': A Tough New Law Meets Reality in L.A. County Courthouses." The lede read: "Courts Toss Curveballs to '3 Strikes'; *Times* study finds only 1 in 6 eligible defendants gets 25 years to life as judges, prosecutors ease sentencing. But many get longer terms than they would have previously." According to the *Times* report, defendants in most of the cases were shoplifters and drug abusers for the ninety-eight cases resolved between March when the law took effect and August 31. Fewer than one in five had been accused of a violent crime. A man who stole diapers from a supermarket was sentenced to eight years in prison. Another was also sentenced to eight years for possession of a rock of cocaine and a bag of marijuana.

Prosecutors were given the discretion to ignore a defendant's past strike in the "furtherance of justice," but judges were not explicitly given that authority. According to the *Los Angeles Times*, "Dist. Atty. Gil Garcetti said in an interview that some of his prosecutors find it traumatic to seek a life sentence for a minor offense, even if a defendant's criminal history is serious. But, he said, prosecutors have to adjust their 'mind set' to the community's growing impatience with business as usual."

Michael's offenses weren't minor. They were very, very serious. He did not, though, have a serious criminal history, but he, too, got swept up in the broad net of the new law.

His older brother, Nicholas, a new father, who served in the Army Reserves and who that day was starting his first job as a security guard, reached Harbor-UCLA hospital soon after Karen did. He remembers that Michael's wound was on the left side of his neck, that there was a patch on his throat, and that Michael was handcuffed to the bed.

"First, I saw him," Nicholas recalls. "Then I saw the hand-cuffs. That's when I knew that this was something serious. I tried to talk to him, but I couldn't. I was just weeping. I was watching him talk to the police. It was the worst day of our lives."

Then Nicholas paused and reversed himself. "No, it wasn't. The worst day of our lives was when he got sentenced."

The judge who had encouraged Michael to plead guilty and who sentenced him was not the same as the one who had decided he should be tried as an adult. This second judge, seeking to soften the blow, ordered that Michael serve his time in the California Youth Authority, the juvenile prison, where those who are sentenced as juveniles can stay until twenty-five. The judge wrote a letter to the prison warden to under-score his request that Michael be kept in juvenile for as much of his twelve years as possible. Instead, Michael was transferred to adult prison the moment he turned seventeen.

13.

WHERE WAS OUR FAMILY?
WHERE WERE THE LAWYERS?

In retrospect, Michael's sentence seems plainly disproportionate—just shy of thirteen years for an attempted robbery,
attempted carjacking, and two successful robberies, all committed by a fifteen-year old within one week and in which the
only person who was physically hurt was himself.

"How could it have happened?" is the first question everyone always wants to ask. Where were the lawyers, they ask?
What did your family do?

Two years earlier, Michael had been hanging out with
a friend named Adam, in Claremont, California, my own
hometown, the archetypal college town where he, his mother,
his sister, and his brother lived at the time. Adam's parents
were house-sitting for the neighbor next door, and the two
thirteen-year-old boys let themselves in with the key and took
a radio. They took it back to Adam's house and sat around listening to it. They must have taken some other items, too. The
neighbor reported a burglary, and when Karen realized that

her boy had done it, she hauled him to the police station. The boys returned everything that they had taken and received in that spring of 1993 a two-year juvenile probation that brought a curfew, but they didn't have to go to court.

In other words, Michael came from family who believed that if you did something wrong, you admitted it, you fixed it, and you suffered the consequences. Even though the matter was far more serious this time round, the attitude was the same. Michael was guilty of the attempted carjacking. There was no pretending otherwise. He was going to have to suffer the consequences.

For reasons that are no longer recoverable, we all, I think, imagined that the consequences would be reasonable. It's worth remembering that the Three Strikes law was still pretty new. It's not as if knowledge about changes in the legal code spreads instantaneously through a population. And it's certainly not the case that the quirks and unintended consequences of any law are quickly recognized. These get discovered in the flesh, as with Michael's life. As with the life of the man who stole diapers, faced a life sentence, and in the end received eight years, an astounding punishment for stealing a $29.99 pack of Huggies.

As it turns out, Karen did have legal advice. Michael was represented by a public defender, an army veteran who had attended L.A. Valley College and then USC. He served as a bailiff in the U.S. Superior Courts before passing the California bar. He was a man who maintained lifelong friendships and, before his death in 2014, had put in thousands of hours as a volunteer at the Little Company of Mary Medical Center in Torrance. I can't tell you what kind of lawyer he was, but Karen thought he had matters in hand.

With regard to family, there were resources to draw on. Karen came from a big family of twelve siblings. They were dispersed, it's true, the East Coast siblings being, at the time, relatively disconnected from those who had struck out for the West. And Karen's father, my grandfather, J. P. Allen, who lived at the time in southern Georgia, certainly didn't have financial resources to contribute. But still, Karen had three brothers in Los Angeles, one sister in Oakland, and another brother, my father, a political science professor, who had a year and a half earlier moved from the Los Angeles area to Michigan. All of them were in a position to help.

Then there was the next generation. I was in England, at Cambridge University, working toward a Ph.D. in classics when Michael was arrested. My brother, Marc, was a senior at Princeton. Michael had visited my parents and brother in Michigan that summer, and my brother showed off to him his brand-new Volkswagen Passat. To this day Marc feels guilty about that interaction, as if it inspired an irrepressible lust for a car. As to Michael's siblings, both Nicholas and Roslyn were trying to make their own post–high school transitions.

So the family—three Los Angeles brothers, my father, and the Oakland sister—were in a position to help. My father, and probably the others, too, offered to help secure legal advice, but Karen thought it wasn't necessary.

In the wake of Michael's arrest, the West Coast family did show up in force for the first set of hearings. And these hearings, it turns out, were the all-important decision point. This is where things might have gone radically differently. These were the hearings that led to the decision as to whether Michael should be charged as a juvenile or as an adult. The judge, a celebrated Hispanic jurist known nationally as a spokesman for minorities in the legal profession, was himself a remarkable family man with seven children of his own who had adopted four more. In a White House ceremony, Ronald Reagan awarded him, his wife, and their children a "Great American Family Award."

At those early hearings, the judge was impressed by Michael's family gathered round. "It's incredible what an excellent support system you have. All of you are here for this young man?" he asked.

But this is also where, from Karen's perspective, everything went wrong. The judge wanted to know what kind of person Michael was. The defense team had no job more important than to prepare witnesses to testify to that question. Karen's sister, Rosyln, or Big Ros, as she was called, wanted to testify about her nephew. She was as close as anyone to Karen and her kids. The family had, from time to time, lived with her. She was also a college-educated activist, who periodically ran for office in the Bay Area on the Peace and Freedom Party ticket. She knew her way around the law and bureaucrats. She was also gay. Because she lived with a woman, she wasn't asked to testify.

It's not clear who worried, this still being the mid-1990s, that her sexual identity would be prejudicial to the case, but someone did. The defense instead called Michael's pastor, Andrew Rinehart, who would, in fifteen years' time, give that off-kilter eulogy at Michael's funeral. Despite the fact that he was thought by parishioners to be a former pimp turned procurer of souls with his own string of convictions, Karen recalls that "it seemed like the 'man of God' of Inglewood would be more profound" than Big Ros.

When Rinehart was called to testify, things took a strange turn. Karen had expected that Rinehart would speak about Michael's psychological profile, which we would now identify as having involved ADHD (attention-deficit/hyperactivity disorder). She thought he would talk about instability in Michael's home life—the family had moved a half dozen times in the previous five years—and she thought that he would talk about the fact that Michael was reaching out and looking for help. She had understood Michael to be doing this with his pastor. Instead, the pastor invoked pastor-parishioner confidentiality and refused to say anything at all about his conversations with Michael. Rinehart was a man who reveled in possessing the secrets of wayward youth, and gave off a vibe that made them feel at home. This must have registered with the judge. Just as he would fourteen years later at Michael's funeral, the pastor here made Michael disappear.

The hearing about whether Michael should be tried as an adult didn't last long. The judge made the decision from the bench. Yes, Michael would be treated as grown.

Probably, this should not have surprised us. The judge made his decision at the high point of the moral panic induced in Angelenos by a welter of terrifying carjackings that saturated the media. In L.A. County, carjackings had nearly doubled from 1991 to 1992, from 3,600 to 6,297. Orange County had its first carjacking in 1992. The defendant in that fatal case was sentenced in May 1994, and the prosecutor recommended the death penalty. A year earlier, the state had passed a bill directly targeting carjacking and establishing stiff penalties. It included the provision that carjacking was an offense for which sixteen-year-olds could be tried as adults. The bill passed unanimously in both houses of the state legislature.

A *Los Angeles Times* article titled "Wave of Fear," appearing the year before Michael's arrest, quoted then Senator Joseph Biden, saying, "Name me a person in L.A. who has a fender-bender and doesn't fear an imminent carjacking. Yes, it's still remote, but you're in the statistical pool now. It's like AIDS. Everyone's in the pool now." Then, in January 1995, California lowered the age at which juveniles could be tried as adults from sixteen to fourteen for a list of twenty-nine violent crimes including carjacking. This was "a list to which the Legislature ke[pt] adding," as the *L.A. Times* put it. And ten days after Michael's own crime, Pete Wilson, the governor of California, signed a bill authorizing the death penalty for people who committed murder during carjackings.

Karen was, however, inside her own story, not the policy story. She knew her boy was still a boy. She expected the hearing to confirm that Michael, as a juvenile offender, should be tried as such. She had entered the hearing fully believing that at its end her baby boy would be released back into her care to await the remainder of his legal proceedings from home. She remembered having taken him to the police about the radio two years earlier and having taken him home again. She had thought that now, too, she would get another chance to take him home. Instead, he was returned, via prison transport, to L.A.'s Central Juvenile Hall, a facility built downtown just before World War I, which, because of unrepaired earthquake damage from the 1994 Northridge quake, was now exposing inmates and staff to asbestos.

At this point, Karen lost her own capacity to function, as did Big Ros, her main support. Big Ros was so devastated that she stopped fighting, and Karen herself spent hours lying on her daybed in the living room in a fetal position. What hurt the most was not being able to touch, not being able to hold her baby. Physical contact wasn't allowed during visiting hours. Yet despite her attenuated ability to function, Karen somehow kept her job. Looking back, she realizes how much her benign bosses supported her. She worked at a social service organization that provided healthcare to the homeless and, looking back, she can see that her employers provided her considerable support.

It is now clear that the extended family didn't gather its forces in the first stage as effectively as it should have. The grown-ups thought we already had the necessary resources on hand: a lawyer who seemed trustworthy, even if assigned by the public defender, a pastor to testify to Michael's character, and a juvenile facing his first arrest. The problem at this stage consisted of both underestimation and overestimation. The family underestimated the level of trouble that Michael was in, because of unfamiliarity with the newly unfolding Three Strikes situation and changing laws concerning juveniles, and the family overestimated the resources that the lawyer and pastor were equipped to provide.

Once it was clear, though, that Michael would be charged as an adult, you might have thought that the family would rally and invest in defense. This did not happen. There was no effort to secure legal representation beyond the public defender, no attempt to challenge the ambulance and hospital bedside confessions, nor any to convert the robbery charge for Smith's watch and wallet into an attempted robbery charge.

There had been a photo lineup for the two robbery charges. Neither victim identified Michael. The second victim began his response to the lineup by saying that none of the photos looked like the person who had robbed him but then in the end averred that perhaps the photo of Michael was closest after all. No work was done to challenge these identifications.

This absence of effort has been something for which I have needed an explanation. Karen's answer is: "As a family, we don't do anything. Everybody effectively raised their family away from everybody. We didn't raise children collectively. So we wouldn't collectively have come together. Family wanted to be present, not necessarily to work on this. Their thinking was, I'll come and show you support, but I don't want to do anything beyond that."

I remember our extended family differently, though. Karen's description of our various nuclear families as living near to one another but also separately, gathering only for holidays or other special occasions, does jibe with my own memory of interactions with the families of my three uncles in Los Angeles and my aunt in the Bay Area, in the last case only because of distance. But it clashes with what I remember of my own family's interactions with Karen and her kids.

My father, a taller, more slender version of Karen, is her older brother, her constant protector. Karen first lived with my mother and father shortly after I was born and shortly after my grandmother—Karen and my dad's mother—had died. It was a brief stay, and she soon moved back home to Florida. But not too many years later, she was back in California with her three children, and my dad routinely helped her as she sought to stabilize her life, and theirs. We five kids—my brother and I and my three cousins of whom Michael was the baby—all spent so much time together as children. When, between 1991 and 1993, Karen and her kids lived in Claremont, the leafy college town where my father taught and my mother was a librarian, they had come to be near us. To this day, my father and Karen remain tightly bound.

About eighteen months before Michael's arrest, my father had moved to Michigan State to take up a deanship there. As I would be a decade later, he was overwhelmingly busy. Yet he spoke regularly with Karen during the months following Michael's arrest. He remembers having tried to figure out how to do what he could to support her, but he also recalls having a sense that there was nothing to be done. Karen says she didn't ask him for help. He was in Michigan. Maybe distance had something to do with it. It's worth noting that in this era just before cell phones, let alone texting, communication was not as routine. Also, during this period, Karen was not terribly good at maintaining a stable phone number.

Distance, though, had never previously stopped my father from helping family. When I was thirteen, on the verge of transitioning from my small private school to the big public high school in our town, I worked one summer filing papers for my father in his overflowing study, and came across nearly illiterate letters, in straining handwriting, from his older sister Cornetta. She had written several times from Orlando to ask for help. They were the anguished letters of a woman routinely beaten and poor as dirt. My father consistently did what he could for her, so why no concerted effort around Michael's defense?

Was it faith in the system or was it ignorance, I've asked them? Was it a faith that God would see them through? Karen gives a different answer. Depression, she said, kicked in so powerfully for her "after it happened." She thinks maybe the hurt and the grief blocked common sense. The simple fact that Michael was still alive, despite the bullet having passed so close to his jugular and his brain stem, was such a pure pleasure that she imagined that the worst of God's wrath had been evaded. Now, Karen says, given what she has learned, she would handle a situation like Michael's completely differently. She would get a private lawyer. She would have done investigations. She would have challenged the hospital bedside confessions made in the absence of any adults. But she also did and does rely on God. "All things work together," she says to punctuate her stories about Michael. "God causes all things to work together for good to those who love God, to those who are called according to His purpose."

All these ingredients form part of the story, yet I still think it boils down to this: Michael came from a family that believes that if you do something wrong, you face the consequences unflinchingly. His family was one that still believed in the reasonableness of the criminal justice system. At each turn, the family learned too late that the criminal justice system was no longer what they thought it was, that its grip was mercilessly tightening, that our son would be but one among many millions soon lost in its vise.

If you hear that the point of the Three Strikes law is to lock up repeat offenders, who is going to think it applies to a fifteen-year-old who has just been arrested for the first time? Who, I ask?

When in nuclear tests bombs are set off underground, they leave a crater on the surface of the earth that will collapse only much later. This, I think, is what the Three Strike laws and the constant upward ratchet in penal severity have been like. In effect, they were a nuclear bomb that went off underground. The people standing on the earth's surface conducted their lives as usual. They figured out what was really going on only after the earth had cratered beneath them.

14.

MILESTONES

The years between ages fifteen and twenty-six are structured with recognizable milestones: high school, driver's license, college, first love, first job, first serious relationship, perhaps marriage, possibly a child.

For those who pass adolescence in prison, none of these rites of passage go away; it's just that they take on a massively distorted shape. It's sort of like a fun-house mirror. These life events don't get ticked off on some sort of regular schedule of progression but get racked up, unpredictably so, over the course of a hard-fought existential struggle. And extra rites of passage, unknown, say, to the high school senior, get added in. First long-term separation from family. First racial melee. First administrative segregation, also known as first solitary confinement. First sodomization.

From the time of his arrest to the time of his sentencing, so for roughly nine months, Michael was mainly, except for a brief transfer to San Fernando, in Central, the juvenile prison.

At Central only parents and legal guardians could visit. This meant that after his arrest, for nine months, he saw his siblings only in court. And visits were brief, thirty minutes after a three-hour wait for admission, in a bare room with nothing but old, gray, stackable office chairs. Parents and children were allowed to hug when the parents arrived and again when they left, but there couldn't be physical contact in between; nor was there a chance to eat together. In these early days, Michael was very emotional, very teary, and very apologetic.

"I didn't mean to hurt you, Mama," Karen remembers him frequently saying.

L.A.'s historic juvenile prison was also like school. The staff sponsored parent meetings that bizarrely had the feel of a PTA. Staff led parents through conversations about why their kids had ended up in Central and about how to support them. They even, PTA-like, gave the parents certificates for their participation. The educational element of Central was serious. Between his arrest in September, at the start of his junior year in high school, and his sentencing in June, Michael earned his GED. By sixteen, in other words, he was a high school graduate. To those who knew him, this was hardly surprising. He was bright and curious. After the sentencing, Michael then transferred to Los Prietos Boys Camp in Los Robles near Santa Barbara. Karen remembers the three-hour drive and taking picnics to Michael. "We had lunch together," she recalls with the trace of a smile. The food, the physical contact, made this camp a high point.

When Michael turned seventeen, he was immediately transferred to a "distribution center" in Kern County, near Fresno. This distribution center in North Kern State Prison takes ninety days to compile inmates' criminal records, life histories, medical and psychological histories, and social relationships, in order to recommend their appropriate institutional placement. They sent seventeen-year-old Michael to the High Desert State Prison in Susanville, near the Oregon state line, one of the toughest prisons in the system.

At this distance, it was impossible for Karen to visit. This was family separation to the max. "That's where," Karen says, "he had his worst experience. He was so new to the prison system." "I could sense it. In my spirit," she continued. "His voice was sad, it was hard to talk sometimes, there was an increase of loneliness, he sounded out of touch, he really needed his family, needed some common ground, something familiar. And I never saw him up there."

Michael would spend his first six months in adult prison without a single family visit. Who knows why the authorities made whatever diagnosis they did that led to Michael's being sent to Susanville. These files remain utterly unavailable.

Devoted mother that she was, and now finally coming out of her own emotional paralysis, Karen started working the phones to get Michael moved closer to home. After those six months, Michael was transferred to dry-as-dust Centinela, across from Mexicali on the Mexican border. For someone driving from Los Angeles, this felt like driving nearly all the way to Yuma, Arizona, where *Shawshank Redemption* happened to be filmed. Karen remembers the exhaustion of the drive and how grateful she was that, having to make an early morning drive on the weekend after a hard week of work, she never ran off the road and into the mountains. Here family sleep-overs were possible, and Karen was able to take her daughter Roslyn, and Roslyn's newborn, Joshua, sick with asthma but nonetheless also playful and happy, to spend time with Michael, who was beginning to adjust to his new life. Numerous scholarly studies agree: family contact is the single most important thing in helping inmates through prison time and back into the world as people less likely to become repeat offenders.

Karen could see Michael starting to change in Centinela, not in his physical appearance but in his demeanor. He was gaining in confidence and settling down. He did vocational courses, gaining certifications in plumbing and electrical work. He joined a Toastmasters club and for the first time in his life overcame his stammer. He converted to Islam.

MICHAEL IN
CENTINELA,
ON PRAYER RUG

Karen says that they didn't talk about prison life in any great detail. She would ask if he was okay, and he would tell her that he was hanging out with older men who were lifers and that they were taking care of him. She met one of these men once, during a visiting day, and then happened to bump into him years later on the outside. He told her then, "Your son is a good son, he just got caught up." These older black inmates kept Michael focused. He did a lot of reading with them and spent time in the library.

The other change that Karen noticed while Michael was in Centinela (the Spanish word for "sentinel") was the arrival of tattoos. Not many. To the very end, Michael had nowhere nearly as many tattoos as the other inmates around him. Some had inked every visible inch of skin and, probably, the rest as well, using pieces and parts from ball point pens and portable CD players to set up ad hoc tattoo parlors. But when Michael left for adult prison, Karen had asked for only one thing— that he *not* get a tattoo. He knew, though, how to forestall her wrath. For his first tattoo, around his wrist, he chose her name, "Karen."

"I never asked for anything else," she recalled. "When I saw my name, I was just furious."

But then, she says, she had a realization. "The one thing I realized was that it was his world now. I couldn't control what was going on. He had to do whatever he had to do to take care of himself."

From Centinela, Michael transferred after three years first to Chino's California Institution for Men and then to the California Rehabilitation Center at Norco. By the time he reached Norco just before 2000, Karen realized that she had seen her boy change from child to man. When he entered Centinela, she remembers, his conversation was full of phrases like "I need" and "Can you send me?" By the turn of the millennium, though, this had shifted.

Now he asked, "Mommy, how are you doing; are you taking care of yourself?"

Although I was eight years older than Michael, by the dawn of the millennium it appeared that he had grown up faster than I. Graduate school prolongs a state of dependence, and I started

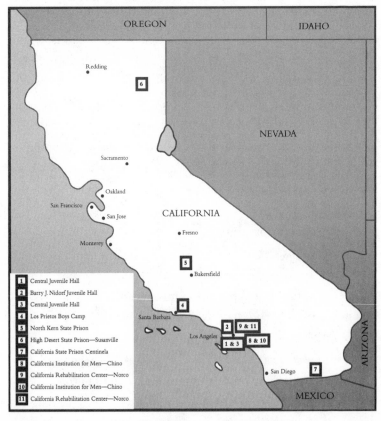

MAP OF PLACES WHERE MICHAEL WAS INCARCERATED

"NORCO, CA STATE PRISON" 2015, PHOTO BY STEPHEN TOURLENTES

my first full-time job only in 1998 at the age of twenty-six. By then, Michael had been in prison, surviving even in an adult facility, for several years. When in 1999 Michael and I picked up a relationship that had lapsed when I left for graduate school in England, we found ourselves closer to being peers than we had been as children. The eight years between us had seemingly diminished to only a few. This gave us the chance to become friends on an equal footing and to confide in each other. He was as shaken as I by my parents' 1999 divorce. The seeming stability of their marriage had been as much of an orienting point for him as it had for me.

When Michael and I reconnected in the late nineties, he was transitioning through Chino—a notoriously tough prison—and landing in Norco, the final stop on his journey. Sometime after I moved to Chicago in January of 1998 to start teaching at the University of Chicago, Michael and I began talking regularly on the phone. Once he moved to Norco, I began to visit him regularly, every other week in the summer, and once or twice during the Christmas holidays, depending on the visiting schedule. The only seasonal differences I remember in those prison visits had to do with the weather: warm or chilly. I don't recall any holiday decorations inside the prison, probably for good reason. Christmas ornaments would surely have made excellent weapons. Over my seven or eight years of visiting Michael, the environment in the visiting area was utterly unchanging.

15.

NORCO

Norco's full name was and is California Rehabilitation Center–Norco, but it's not clear how much genuine rehabilitation was on offer during the years that Michael was there. It was among the state's older prisons, having been built in 1928 as the Lake Norconian Club, an actual luxury hotel, on an actual lake. Its focus was supposed to be on drug and alcohol rehabilitation, and during discussions of possible prison closures in 2005, its warden defended it on the basis of the quality of its drug treatment program. But Michael didn't need that sort of rehabilitation, and the prison didn't offer much beyond that. There was the obligatory poorly stocked library but few classes or, at least, nothing past the GED level. College and university classes were all scrapped in the 1990s because of budget cuts, and in 1996 the state and federal government ceased providing prisoners access to Pell Grants for correspondence courses. Higher education, once seen as an antidote to recidivism, had been reconceived as a privilege that inmates had not earned.

There were jobs to be had: kitchen (bad) and working on paperwork for inmate reception and release (better). Michael had a radio in his cell, and he could purchase toiletries and snacks at the prison canteen, with funds from his minimal earnings or money orders sent by family. We all sent money periodically—Karen, my father, my brother, me. Probably other cousins, too. We knew he was often hungry; the meals were bland and insufficient. But whenever he got a money order, he would binge on items from the canteen even though he had actually wanted the funds to pay for a steady supply of extra snacks.

Theft was a perennial problem in the prison and exacerbated the feast-or-famine habits of poverty. When Michael bought a new round of snacks, like Pop-Tarts or burritos, he was afraid that he would lose them; that they'd be stolen, and then, if he hadn't already eaten them, that he would just have nothing. So he ate everything all at once when he got it. There was a limit, though, on how often a prisoner could receive a money order or package, so once he'd binged, he had to go hungry for weeks. Once, we worked it out to send him double the money so that he could buy two sets of snacks, hiding one set away to be his permanent backup. The idea was that, if he had the reassurance of a backup supply, it would be easier for him to resist the urge to eat all of his snacks immediately. I'd gotten the idea from some sociological studies of poverty I'd been reading. This worked for a few months. He was able to pace himself. But then he wasn't, or maybe the backup pack got scented out by another inmate and stolen. I don't really know what happened to that plan, but in the end the feast-or-famine rhythm won.

Michael would call at least once a week, sometimes more often, except for when the prison was on lockdown because of outbreaks of violence. Then you might go weeks without hearing from him. I was a good phone partner because I could afford the astronomical collect-call charges from the phone company. Every call began with a reminder, a robotic voice saying, "This is the California Department of Corrections. Will you accept the charges?" And then, every fifteen seconds, as if we could forget, there was another recorded interruption: "This call has originated from a California State Prison."

Michael always called because he needed contact, which meant that if he called and you were there you needed to make time. Very often this brought great joy. It was always a relief to hear Michael's voice again, to hear that (usually) he still sounded more or less like himself, and that life went on. Sometimes, though, it was also hard to need to be available at whatever point Michael got his chance to call.

My first husband, Bob, then a professor of poetry at the University of Chicago and a lover of boxing, did a lot for Michael, something for which I will always be grateful. He was always ready to step in if I couldn't do a whole call at the moment the phone rang. If I wasn't home, Michael would speak to Bob. If Bob wasn't home, he would speak to my stepson, Isaac, with whom Michael was playing chess by snail mail, one move every few weeks. Like everyone else who knew Michael, Isaac, too, developed a great fondness for him, and Michael loved having someone to teach.

Michael had a lot of correspondents, actually, and each of us probably had a completely different relationship with him. For my stepson, it was all about chess. For Mother H., the wife of the pastor at one of Michael's family's churches, it must have been about God. Once he moved to Norco, Michael converted from Islam back to Christianity and started leading Bible study classes. I think the motivation to convert had mainly to do with where in the prison he thought he was mostly likely to find people with whom to live a more settled, stable life in a world where violence and conflict were otherwise the daily staple. But he wept when Mother H. died, so there was something deeper there, too, something we never discussed.

With my husband and me, the conversation was generally about school, reflecting the overwhelming philosophy of the extended family. Michael desperately wanted to go to college. He had a lively mind and wanted, above all, to learn French. My family had lived in France for a year, the year before Michael was born, and we sometimes spoke French at home. Somehow that lodged in him deeply. Learning French was one of his life goals. He tried in high school and tried again in prison.

I not only respected but revered Michael's desire to learn. I didn't care whether it was French, Malayalam, medieval architecture, or the history of the Black Panthers. Getting him into college became my single most intense aspiration. I believe in education. I believed in Michael. To myself I did not formulate my pursuit of this goal in any way clearer or more definite than that. I just know with every fiber of my being that education makes life better. Period. My parents had always told me that when I graduated from high school, I could get a job or go to college. If the latter, they would help me; if the former, I would be on my own. Either way, after I finished studying, they would have nothing else to leave me because they would have already given me everything in giving me an education.

> Dear Isaac,
>
> This is Michael. Although we have not met I feel as if I already know you. I've heard a lot about you and will enjoy the time when we finally meet. Until then I will tell a little about myself with you. My full name is Michael Alexander Allen. I play basketball and football. I also like running track. I want you to know that whatever questions you may have, that you are more then welcome to ask me. In the mean time I would like to play you in a game of chess. I enjoy chess for many reasons. One of those reasons is that it trains the mind to make the best choice possible. What I will do is draw a diagram of a chess board and it's pieces on paper. Danielle will make copies of the game moves along. I will send the diagram to give you the first move, if you choose to play. I hope to meet you soon and I will be waiting to hear from you, chess game or not. Until pen and paper meet again, Take Care—
>
> Sincerely,
> Michael

LETTER FROM MICHAEL TO ISAAC, THE AUTHOR'S STEPSON

(Perhaps this is why I have never left school!) With the same ferocity of purpose, I sought to do the same for my own baby, my little cousin. I suppose it matters, too, that at this point, married to a much older man, who already had two sons, I did not expect to have children of my own.

I started off, of course, in my usual way. I undertook the obligatory research to figure out how getting Michael a college degree might be possible. On November 8, 2001, only eight weeks after September 11, Michael mailed me his application to Indiana University's Program in General Studies, and I mailed it onward with a check. Allens both, we aimed high. We aimed for the bachelor's degree in general studies. The day he was admitted to start with the January 2002 sequence of classes was as exhilarating as the day I received my own fat envelope from Princeton thirteen years earlier. World events were at a great distance from Norco. As the rest of the country was pivoting to a war footing, we were getting ready to go to school.

Michael was interested not only in French but also in philosophy and literature. Each department had appealing introductory classes, but there was a catch. No hardcover books were allowed into the prison. Michael could enroll only in classes for which the textbooks had soft covers. I had to make another round of phone calls. It turned out that, with this filter, French was out as was Introduction to Philosophy. The choices that remained were Intro to Ethics and Intro to Writing and Study of Literature. Michael chose Lit 141 with Professor Donald J. White, an earnest teacher who gave even his incarcerated students extensive and astute feedback. I paid the fees and ordered the books and, for Michael, something new began.

New Year's came and so did the *Bible*, the *Odyssey*, the *Inferno*, the *Canterbury Tales*, and the *Persian Letters*. But it didn't go well. Michael had trouble completing the assignments. There were distractions, of course—racial melees, Bible study, work in the office. For whatever reason, Michael couldn't quite get traction with the reading; he could not secure an oasis for reflection and focus. At some point in the year, Bob and I came to the conclusion that doing college in prison was unlikely to work for Michael. Conversations had started in the family about where Michael should go in four years' time when he got out. We hadn't yet learned about the requirement that he parole to the county where he committed his crime, and, in conversations with Karen, Bob and I volunteered to have him come to Chicago to live with us and go to school. Bob was deeply involved, as I mentioned, with the world of boxing, and closely tied to a black gym on the Southside. We had any number of young men passing through our house, seeking help of one kind or another. We'd been fostering one young homeless teenager, and had helped him get to college. We thought we could do the same for Michael.

We hadn't shared this with him yet. Then, in late September 2002, we stopped hearing from him. This is a routine feature of corresponding with an inmate, and there's little you can do. If the inmate has died, you'll learn about it. Otherwise, it's very hard to extract information from the prison itself. It's radio silence until the inmate gets an opportunity to get a message out, officially or unofficially.

In early November, we learned why we hadn't heard from Michael. Another "racial melee" had broken out at Norco, and Michael had been sent to the nearby Chino prison pending the completion of an investigation into his alleged participation in the incident. Norco didn't have facilities for "Administrative Segregation" or, in more ordinary parlance, solitary confinement, hence the transfer to Chino. After a month in "the hole,"

"CHINO, CA STATE PRISON" 2015, PHOTO BY STEPHEN TOURLENTES.

as inmates called it, without his property, including his address book, and without even paper and pencil, he was found not guilty and was finally able to write.

The relevant evidence for finding him not guilty had been gathered right at the beginning of the process: "Several of us were randomly picked because no participants could be identified. I had an old abrasion under my eye from playing basketball. The nurse confirmed the abrasion was sealed and was presently healing, meaning the scar was older than one hour." Yet still he was in the hole for a month.

Inmate family chat sites yield the following sort of advice for when your "man is in the hole":

YOU MIGHT WANT TO SEND HIM STAMPS, ENVELOPES AND PAPER AND ALSO ANY ADDRESSES THAT HE MAY

NOT BE ABLE TO REMEMBER BY HEART BECAUSE HE
WONT HAVE ANY OF THAT WITH HIM-GOOD LUCK
AND HANG IN THERE!

Large-scale race fights in the prison would put the prison
on lockdown multiple times of year. They could result in one
or another racial group being punished with a restriction of
visits. Michael once confided to me that he had a "melee" partner, a Latino inmate with whom, when fights broke out, he in
essence danced so that they could make it look as if they were
fighting each other. The "melees" could involve all three major
racial groups in the prison simultaneously—white, black, and
Latino—or only two of those groups. Any number of things
might trigger a melee—from a crosswise word or look, to a
killing on the outside that needed to be revenged on the inside.
The political dynamics of prisons are complex.

Sometime during his time in "the hole" in Chino, he did
get a letter from my father, Uncle William, sharing the news
of the proposal for him to move to Chicago to live with Bob
and me. Michael wrote us a long letter in response:

I received a letter from Uncle William and he
told me that he had spoken with you. As you know,
probably, I was unable to complete the course. I
cannot fully blame my most recent situation [the
administrative segregation]. Prior to the incident, I was
doubting myself. I became unsure of myself and was
scared that I would fail. Not just myself but my family
who is putting a lot of love, trust, and faith in me.
Faith which I sometimes lack in myself. During the

time I was isolated, I recognize that I was wallowing
in self-pity. For no apparent reason except that it
distracted me from giving thought to what's outside
these walls. Though my need, desire, and wanting
to come home is overwhelming, I am half afraid that
I will not succeed. I overestimated myself and was
disappointed with the results I was getting from my
class. . . . I had thought that I was prepared but that
was another overestimation. . . . But in all honesty,
I was never prepared (mentally or emotionally) for
what you did for me. Three years ago I had given up
on taking college courses and settled with the idea
that I would have to wait until I came home. Now
Uncle William tells me that you and Bob would like
for me to stay with you and start a new life going to
college. For several days I was speechless. I was only
able to write Uncle William due to the necessity of
my situation. Outside of that I was paralyzed with
happiness. I was confused because I didn't understand
it. I didn't do anything to deserve such a generous
gesture of love. And it is for this reason I am confident
and content in my ability to make something of
myself. No matter the circumstances, I can do it. It's
simple. I have to do it. . . . I would like to repeat the
Lit 141 class again. I have all the books and I know that
I am ready. I've learned much over the past year, and I
know I can apply it correctly. Before I send this letter,
I want to ask if you have finished writing your book,
Talking to Strangers. I hope you have been able to further
your writing. . . . Love always, Michael.

Bob and I did not see ourselves as doing something worthy of this degree of gratitude. I was crushed that Michael could not imagine taking an invitation such as the one we were making for granted. Still, I was glad that he wanted to come, and I was glad not just for his sake. Michael and I were on our way to becoming writing partners. I would tell him about my efforts with my academic books. I would test out arguments on him.

Did he know, I would ask, that Elizabeth Eckford, one of the Little Rock Nine, who had tried to integrate Central High School in Little Rock, Arkansas, in 1957, had sewn her own dress for the first day of school? Onto the bottom section of her full-skirted dress, she had sewn a band of black-and-white checked fabric. Her dress, I said, was a flag flown for her own vision of integration. How brutally she was received by the segregationist crowds when she walked alone to school that day. Her family, which didn't have a phone, had not gotten the message that the kids were to assemble early that morning and make the way to school as a group, escorted by ministers and police. Turned away from the school, by the National Guard, Elizabeth walked, shoulders bowed, seeking safety, and, in the trauma, slipped into a silence that lasted for days. Flying her flag for integration, she had been ready to make a sacrifice—to submit herself to the barrage—for a higher purpose, but this country took too much.

When Michael asked me about my own writing, he was asking me what I needed, how I was doing, if I was tending to my own flame, just as he would ask his mother if she was taking care of herself.

Now he was ready to try again at his own writing. Once

ELIZABETH ECKFORD TURNING AWAY FROM HOSTILE CROWDS
OUTSIDE OF CENTRAL HIGH SCHOOL IN LITTLE ROCK, ARKANSAS,
SEPTEMBER 4, 1957

more, we set off on Lit 141, and this time Michael turned out
one gem of an essay after another, readings of those epic texts
that were full of insight and personal connection to the ancient
stories. He didn't turn these essays out quickly. He did it at
something like two-to-four-month intervals, but he got it
done. He was finding his voice. Reading and writing released
him to speak; his voice took wing like a butterfly. The stam-

mer, now nearly gone in his speech, never showed up on the page. To watch a voice emerge, as from a chrysalis, is a beautiful thing, a teacher's greatest privilege.

This is how I came to know that for him prison was, in his own words, an Inferno.

16.

INFERNO, IN MICHAEL'S WORDS

TWO HELLS:
IN SURVIVAL, FINDING ONE'S SELF

There was a time I had never thought of Hell outside of Christianity. I had never heard of the *Odyssey* and only heard of the *Inferno* from watching Jeopardy. Since reading these two books life for me has an added new meaning. For instance: Dante's Inferno creates an all too detailed visualization of Hell and what it may be. While reading the *Inferno* I've often put myself behind Virgil and Dante walking through Hell. I don't take kindly to seeing myself in Hell, but Dante's writing makes it impossible to just read without visualization. In my opinion Hell is under-rated. It is not taken seriously, even by people who say they believe in God or, as some candy coat it, a higher power. The Inferno reminds vividly of a culture that I have been religiously a part of for over the past 7 years. It is the life I live in Prison which to me is Hell. In many ways prison is like Hell. There are differences but they do not underscore the Hellish reality of Prison.

The Inferno is constructed like a prison. It is especially similar to the eighth circle. The souls are in pits which are guarded by beasts and demons. They are being punished in accordance to their sins on earth. Prison is the same way. The sins we committed as citizens are judged according to law which is based on universal principles. We, who are in prison, had to answer for our sins and our lives were taken from us. Our bodies became the property of the state of California. We are reduced to numbers and stripped of our identity. To the state of California I am not Michael Alexander Allen but I am K-10033. When they want to know anything about me they do not type my last name in the computer but it is my number that is inputted. My number is my name. I am K-10033. In the *Inferno* those who are inquired of are asked [their names]. Here is one of the differences between my hell in prison and the *Inferno*. The souls in the Inferno are called by name. To some, it may be a matter of filing but to me, it is a means to keep anyone with the potential to be great, mentally enslaved.

The suffering in prison is almost an exact replica of circle six, the 2nd ring. Those who were violent against themselves are without identity. Because they committed violence on their own selves they are without bodies. Instead, they are imprisoned in trees and bushes. They bleed in pain when so much as a branch is broken or a bush is trampled by dogs. So it is the same with inmates who are tried and tested every day.

Inmates bleed when they are unable to protect themselves. They become trees, susceptible to abuse and left writhing in pain, mentally and physically.

The suffering varies in prison. Mentally, the suffering is unbearable. It's a constant beating on my sanity. My emotions feel as if they're in a river full of tears, raging with unfed paranhas. I think of circle 4 when the hoarders and wasters are pushing weight against each other. This struggle is done for an eternity. I'm left with thoughts of never making it out because that which I struggle against is at most times incomprehensible. The subjection and oppression my mind takes seems to be an eternity. I think of Dante's use of ice as nothing but a mere deception. Ice within itself is enticing to the burning soul. Ice can get so cold that it burns flesh. And it's parallel to any sin committed on earth. The root of sin is lust and the desire to satisfy that lust. Lust becomes a sin when it is against human Nature. Lust only creates wanting and wanting creates greed and greed burns Flesh. It is lust that causes us to believe we have to have something at all cost. This is my suffering, this is my hell. 24 hours all night. There is no day. My soul in its entirety is in darkness.

Ice is Dante's enticing deception. Deception is darkness. Whichever lust (ice) that convinced me I needed something at all cost, was my deception and therefore the reason for my present darkness. My present darkness is this prison. A culture of hellish existence that I have suffered over the past 2,700 days. There is no sure thing as surviving, just barely existing. My lust is like the hoarder of circle 4. My flesh is like the wasters who are fighting against the hoarders in circle 4. Internal light cannot be extinguished except by the possessor thereof.

Virgil is my internal light. I accept and build on whatever rea-
soning I can comprehend from Virgil (my subconscious). I'm
trapped in a hell with whom society decrees to be the worst of
living and better off dead. Robbers, rapists, child molesters,
carjackers, murderers, and dope fiends who would spend their
mother's monthly rent for a quick fix. And here I am, amongst
them. As much as the mere thought disgusts me, I am one of
them. Just another number, not deserving of a second chance.
In this hell where I have lived with thousands of different, nasty,
confused, perverted, sorry, pathetic, evily slick, and heartless
wraiths, I do have a second chance. In this hell, where I have
come across dozens of Virgils, Shakespeares, Martin Luther
King Jr.s, Einsteins, Alex Haleys, and Dantes, I have a second
chance. In this hell I am Dante. Dante was not in hell due to a
fatal sin but somewhere in his life he strayed onto the path of
error, away from his true self. I, K-10033, strayed away from
my true self: Michael Alexander Allen.

And like Dante I am forced to descend lower into hell to
achieve a full awakening. I am forced into depression, scarred
by obscenities, war after war, but each war that I survive I am
a step closer to a full awakening of self. My hell is no longer
demonstrating what I am capable of doing in order to survive.
It has become what I can tolerate and withstand in order to
live. I cannot help but to judge those around me. I am one of
them but we are far from the same. Like Dante I am cursed
with a spirit of discernment which allows us to see the truth
for what it is. There are most whom I despise who are truly
sick beyond healing and they should never leave this place.
Then there are those who await to fulfill their destiny. I see
in them a sincere and apologetic heart for their ill misdeeds.

They are the one who will change the world positively or positively change someone's world. Hell cannot hold the latter of the two opposites but in time will only spit them back out into society to do what is right. The hell that I live in cannot hold Dante. Hell can test and try one's self but it cannot hold Dante and it will not hold me. In the *Inferno*, the dead are trapped forever. Surely, the biggest and most important difference in the Inferno and my hell called prison, is that I have a way out.

17.

VISITING 1.0

If many of my memories of Michael's time in prison involve coaching him over the phone through his writings about canonical texts, a good portion of the rest involve long visits with him and, most often, with my aunt Karen, in Norco's barebones visiting room and prison yard. These visits possessed an emotional rhythm: the sense of steeling yourself against the difficult as you started the early morning drive from L.A., the rising anticipation as you got closer; the quiet joy of the visit; and the aching disappointment that inevitably came with departure, with leaving one's loved one still inside.

Once one arrived at the prison, visits had an intensely ritualistic quality, the underlying purpose of which is control. You might want to say control of the inmates or control of their families, but that wouldn't seem quite right. The target of the rituals felt more indiscriminate. The object is simply control in its own right.

As Michael, known to the system as K-10033, wrote,

AERIAL PHOTO OF CALIFORNIA REHABILITATION CENTER—NORCO

inmates went by numbers, not names, and visiting days were
allocated to sets of numbers. Half of the evens on one Saturday. Half of the odds on Sunday. The other halves of each set
the following week. Before you could even begin to visit, you
first had to apply for permission to enter. You had to get your
name "on the list." This could take months. And then the visits
themselves were odysseys. We generally set out at about four
or five in the morning, in the half-dark of predawn, and drove
straight toward the rising sun, in order to get to the prison by
6:30 A.M. There we would join the line of waiting cars snak-
ing from the parking lot past a row of suburban baseball fields
that bordered the prison. This was a good time for heart-to-
hearts between Karen and me. What were her aspirations for
her ministry? Who did she have living on her couch and why?

What was happening with my marriage to Bob? There was a funny story about an earthquake hitting while she was high from a time, decades earlier, before she'd gotten sober. If we went on a Saturday, there would often be Little League games in play as we drove away past the fields in the afternoon.

At 7:30 A.M. the guards would let a parade of Kias and Hyundais, Chevys and Dodges, into the parking lot, and then you would sign in at a lectern at the front of a canopied structure with wooden benches that looked something like a tent revival meeting. Hosts of mainly black and brown women, but white women, too, and many children, and some men, flitted in the shadows under the canopy. We could take in up to $30 in quarters or singles in plastic Baggies, and we always took the maximum. The point of this was to purchase treats for the inmates from the row of vending machines dispensing, as it turned out, quite disgusting microwaveable cheeseburgers and burritos along with mystery meat plates.

It also mattered how you dressed. You couldn't wear blue denim because that's what the inmates wore. You couldn't wear beige or khaki because that's what the guards wore. You couldn't wear tight clothes or clothes that showed cleavage or skirts shorter than two inches above the knee or sleeves shorter than two inches below the shoulder. If you were dressed wrong, you weren't let in. You always took a backup set of clothes, just in case.

If there was a focal point of the control, I suppose it was the attempt to target desire. The lines of women who lined the benches under the canopy of the faux revivalist meeting pushed back. In an inmate family chat room, one wife wrote:

I always dress up like i am going on a hot date . . . cause i am

. . . with my hubby!!! :D I usually wear a dress and high heels . . . just make sure the dress is no more than two inches above the knee . . . this is true even if you wear leggings underneath. When i wear pants, I usually go with dark black jeans or black or chocolate color slacks or pedal pushers (they show off the heels real good;)) with a pretty top. Pink and purple are always safe choices. I wear red a lot. . . . Do your lips right before your process in and he will be drooling the second he lays eyes on you!!;) Have fun lady!!:

And another chimed in:

I must say I agree with Hisprettygirl and Jackjack—I always dress to impress because I like to remind him what he's got waitin for him at home;)

Karen and I always kept it pretty basic and simple, loose-fitting pants and comfortable T-shirts or sweaters. We weren't really the objects of the policy. We were there to see a son, a cousin, not a lover.

After the waiting, the signing in, and the clothing check, one waited again until a guard called the number of the inmate you happened to be visiting. Then, all at once, the eight-foot-tall metal gates underneath the front guard tower would roll open, clanging, and let you into a small pen.

The gates would then clang again, snapping behind you now, like a drawbridge, and then another set of gates in front of you would open, to let you onto a short walkway that led into the nondescript processing room, a stand-alone hut-like structure, its interior like any other undecorated, institutional waiting room. There you'd wait again and then hand over your ID and your Baggie filled with coins and single bills to be checked, before receiving your pass and proceeding through a metal detector into the prison yard, a scant place with little vegetation and scraggly grass, to cross over a short walkway to the visiting hall.

Entering the hall, the smell of bleach would wash over you. To your right was another guard station, this one a raised booth. There was a row of vending machines directly across from the guard station. You'd reach up to the guards to hand over your pass, and they would phone the dormitories to call your inmate for his visit. If you'd gotten into the line of cars early, the room would be empty, filled with only low round tables and small chairs, like the kind they have in kindergartens. If you'd gotten into the line of cars late, you'd enter a room already swimming with men in blue jeans, blue shirts, and tattoos, each with a little circle of color surrounding him, the whole space incongruously like a small Italian piazza full of merrily buzzing café tables.

You'd spend your time talking, trying to avoid eating crap, or, if the weather was decent, you'd spend the time outside, walking in tight circles in the yard or sitting at a picnic table. Sometimes you would get your picture taken all together by a guard serving as prison photographer, who stood on duty snapping one Polaroid after another. There were a handful of board games around for the kids. Now and then the loudspeaker would sound for the count—every inmate in the prison had to be counted every so often—and all the men would file off, emptying the room, only to return twenty or thirty minutes later. You would stay for three or four hours and it would feel like a blink of an eye when they called your inmate back to his cell.

Then you would reverse your itinerary to the exit. Past the vending machines and raised guard station. Out the door.

Across the scraggly grass. Through the metal detector. Wave to the guards in the processing room. Wait for the guards up above to open the pen. Into the pen. Wait for the guards up above to close the gate behind you and open the gate in front of you. Listen to it clank behind you, the drawbridge shutting yet again. I'm not sure if we ever waved at the guards in the front tower. I don't think so. But maybe we did now and then.

In the early afternoon, you would drive away past the baseball games, echoing with the cheers of what looked like happy suburbanites, and if you had managed to avoid eating any of the microwaveable junk from the vending machines, you'd turn the corner from the prison and drive a couple of blocks into town to have a meal at Wendy's or Burger King. They were a major step up from what was on offer in Norco. And then you would head back to Los Angeles, quiet most of the way, drained and defeated once again.

You never once would have seen the lake beside which the luxury hotel was built in 1928, although they were both still there. The hotel now serves as the women's prison, visible up on the hill above the parking lot and looking grand, like some old-time mansion.

By this point in his incarceration, Michael seemed "secure in himself" to Karen. His mother could tell that he was proud of his accomplishment with his college classes, and she was relieved that he never turned into a tough. "No, he didn't get tough in prison," she recalled, adding, "Later he got tough for the lifestyle he wanted to live; but in prison he was still gentle, smiling, Michael." He got tough during his second stint, for his parole violation, and in those final months of his life. But in Norco, not yet.

Michael did become, Karen says, "a little more lax, less wound up, a little cocky." She tells a story about one disappointing visit. "I'll never forget, they'll call him in for a count. He goes out. I wait and he doesn't show. One of his buddies tells me, he's not coming back out because he had chewing gum in his mouth." She lost the rest of her visit with her son that day because he'd gotten cocky.

But he never turned into a tough, although there were plenty of those to be seen in that visiting room.

18.

VISITING 2.0

Time for my own confession. I wrote that last chapter like an academic. Which I am. The description of visiting that I gave you wasn't about me. It was about some disembodied "you." To write that chapter, I stepped into the perspective of an outside observer, the luxury afforded to academics when they travel the world encountering pain and injustice. To be an academic is to acquire an excuse for not owning the pain you see.

Take a look at what I wrote:

"Visits had an intensely ritualistic quality, the underlying purpose of which is control. You might want to say control of the inmates or control of their families, but that wouldn't seem quite right. The target of the rituals felt more indiscriminate. The object is simply control in itself."

Abstraction. Distancing. Those are my first tools of self-protection. Athena's spear and shield.

I will have to try again to describe what visiting Michael meant to me.

The fact that I told the story as an academic already tells you everything you need to know. That wound of visiting Michael in prison goes so deep that somehow, even in writing this book, I have found it hard to own up to one simple fact. I went to prison. I was in prison.

No, I don't mean that I have been arrested or convicted of a crime. I have avoided that because thus far in life I have had that combination of goods that the ancient Greek philosopher Aristotle thought was necessary for a happy life: resources, decent character, and luck.

My father and mother gave me the first two items from that treasure chest. The Lord, my God, whom I believed in as a child, and then did not believe in, and then came to believe in again as I emerged from periods of great pain, has given me the third.

All right. So now you know more about me than anybody other than my husband, my second husband, that is. Our wedding took place barely a month before Michael's murder.

But, no, I was not in prison as a convict, and this is thanks to my father, my mother, and my God. Yet even as someone who could come and go, I felt the prison's mark, its branding fork. I felt it in my soul, even though all I was, there, was a day's sojourner.

What exactly did I feel? The women were gloriously flamboyant in their dress. Not me. I'm a bookworm and more or less dress like one. A lot of black, now and then some bright color. But for these prison trips I probably pretty much always wore all black. Black T-shirts, black linen pants. Tennis shoes. You have to do something to lift your spirit up when you go into the prisons. I didn't do it with clothes. I did it with conversation. I understand the show, the color, the make-up. But I wasn't there to visit a boyfriend. I was there to visit an Allen. One proud member of a proud family come to see another, both of us trying to pretend we had not been broken. We talked about ideas—about books and people; about freedom and politics.

To explain why I was there in that prison, I could try to say that Allens have a fierce bond and that we stick by our own. This would be right and wrong at the same time. The right part about that story has to do with our all being sprung from J. P. Allen, north Floridian island fisherman turned Baptist preacher, patriarchal head of a sprawling family, half of it official, half of it enjoyed in secret. For this reason, J. P.'s progeny extended to a cousinage that adds up to an uncountable number. Yet there is surely not a one of us from either the official or the secret branch who does not have in our soul the sights and sounds of tall, bald, lean, and leonine J. P. thundering from a church pulpit in gorgeous gospel baritone:

> *He's a battle axe*
> *In the time of battle*
> *He's a battle axe*
> *In the time of battle*
> *He's a shelter*
> *In the time of storm*

We are fighters, we Allens. And sometimes we fight with each other. That's where the idea that Allens just stick together breaks down. The whole tribe is full of its broken branches, but for those who haven't fallen into fights, the bond is adamantine. My father and his sister, Michael's mother, have had that permanent bond.

We Allens are also an upright people. The Allens have incredible posture, and this is not an accident. We are free people. We have been free a long time, even if one of our forefathers was also, briefly, enslaved through deceit and trickery.

When I went to visit my cousin in prison, I did not feel like a free person. The reason for this is very simple. In that prison, even as only a sojourner, I was not a free person.

Every element of my dress, behavior, affect and time was controlled. Visiting Michael in prison, I learned to say, "Yes, ma'am," and "Yes, sir," to people in authority. I still do it, although now as a sort of inside joke to myself, as a favor to the person whom I so address. It's a favor because I am free, and I don't have to say that, and so now it is a way of gently ennobling them, rather than of expressing any submission.

So who am I and why did I help my cousin? I am an Allen. Some branches of the Allens just do help Allens. My father helped his sister Karen, my cousin's mother. I, my father's daughter, help Karen's children, the cousins I grew up with. It is just what we do. They help me, too. They know me. They've known me since childhood. They take pleasure in my accomplishments and laugh at my foolishness.

To help my cousin, among other things, I went to prison, which it turns out, hurt me even more than I had realized, and

which fact perhaps explains why other members of our imme-
diate family were not able to make those trips.

When May rolled round, Michael always sent his mother
a Mother's Day card. During his last few years in prison, he
always sent me one, too.

You try it sometime, going to prison, even just for a day.
There are lots of people who need visits but don't get any.

19.

DIZZY

After Michael got out of the hole in the fall of 2002, he gave his Indiana University college course another try. By six months in, just past spring break season, Michael was making good progress—worrying about his upcoming midterm like any other college student. With regard to jobs inside prison, though, he'd gotten stuck. He had been trying to put himself forward for the better jobs, desk jobs instead of kitchen jobs or physical labor. In quick succession, for reasons he didn't know, he'd failed to get two jobs that he really wanted. But somehow in the course of those efforts, he learned from a supervisor that he might be eligible for the inmate firefighting crew that Norco sponsored for the California Department of Forestry. The inmates were trained to tackle California's fearsome wildfires, and joining the fire camp would mean time outside the prison.

Only "Level 1" inmates, however, could be assigned to fire

camp. These were inmates without a "violent" code in their file, and Michael was not one of these. He'd been coded "violent" when he first went to prison because of the nature of his offense. But an attentive supervisor helped him realize that, on account of his youthfulness upon arrest and his behavior since he had been in prison, he ought to be eligible to get the "violent" code removed. And so it transpired that in May of 2003, at his annual review, Michael was downgraded. His spirit leapt. For the first time in a long time, he had something to look forward to.

Days later, Michael got to go outside. He got assigned to fire camp on May 19, 2003, his first day outside of prison or a prison transport vehicle in almost eight years. The training involved learning to hike in and out of canyons, how to cut "firelines," the breaks in fuel sources that are supposed to stop a greedy fire in its tracks. He learned how to use shovels and rakes for this work, and learned crew roles like captain, swamper, and dragspoon. He recorded those first four days.

5-19-03

DAY 1—I felt real dizzy. I've always thought I would be acutely aware of everything on that first day. I felt myself panic. For an instant I even wanted to run back inside. The free air had me coughing alot. Going up the mountain I saw the sky was noticeably different from in prison. Even though it has been the same sky since the beginning of time. I really started to take a lot in going down the mountain. Yellow small flowers lined the trail. There were purple ones as well.

5-20-03

DAY 2 — I noticed the trees this time. I saw them on day 1 but this morning they seemed to speak to me "look at me." My mouth actually watered in desire never to leave the trees' side. When I got up the mountain I noticed people were around. I was in awe observing life outside of prison. I pictured people going to work, school, or even shopping. It made me groan inside.

5-21-03

DAY 3 — I saw people horse riding. Other guys were laughing because the ladies were overweight and they mocked feeling sorry for the horse. I felt sick because these guys were making jokes as if they were better than them. I thought at least they can do what they want when they want.

5-22-03

DAY 4 — I was irritated and partly distracted as a result of eating prunes earlier this morning. I won't do that again. On the way back I found myself feeling depressed. Even as I write I feel my eyes teary. It is a blessing to be able to leave and come back. But, it hurts to leave knowing I'll come back.

During this stretch of time, something else big happened. Michael fell in love. I remember a phone call. I can't remember precisely when it was. But I remember his words, "I've met someone, Danielle. She's beautiful." I remember my sense of utter confusion. "Met someone? How? Where?" I couldn't compute how Michael could have met a woman. Was it a guard he'd met? There were women guards in the visiting room whom I'd gotten to know over my visits. But in some sort of fumbling way, we came to understand each other. Michael had fallen in love with a fellow inmate, a man named Isaiah with implants or hormone-induced breasts who dressed and lived as Bree. She was, he said, unquestionably the most beautiful woman in the prison.

He hadn't told his mother, but he told me, and he wanted me to promise to say nothing. He knew his mother would be upset and he feared she would judge him. He hoped I wouldn't.

I didn't judge him. I suppose there was a twinge of surprise, but I didn't really reflect on the specifics of the relationship. I loved my lesbian aunt, Big Ros, and her partner had done my hair throughout my middle school years. I was used to going with the flow of people's sexual identities. Nor did I ask about what Bree had done to land in Norco. Michael and I never spoke about what any of his fellow inmates had done to land in prison and this case was no exception. I didn't learn until after Michael's death what Bree was in for. I just accepted that Michael had found someone inside who seemed to mean something to him and make him happy and I was glad. I didn't address any of my reflections to any sort of imagined future. I reacted only to the present, and Michael's voice on the phone was content in a way that I had never heard. I wanted him to have that.

Like freedom, desire was dizzying to Michael. A month

later, Michael sent me a piece of writing unlike anything else he ever sent me. "The world has change and brothas far from the same," he rapped and continued:

> *Am I losing my mind*
> *No; I think I found it*
> *Realizing greatness in one's self is very astounding*
> *and truth be told, I recognize a King*
> *cause when I look in the mirror all I see is me*
> *And us, so please trust, we can't be touch*
> *standing together forever is a necessary must.*

Soon enough, he sent me Bree's annual prison shot. She was posed as a woman, lying on the floor like a sports pinup, made up and in colorful clothing. Bree was beautiful or, at least, in that territory, and certainly ready to compete with Hisprettygirl and Jackjack, the women who sought to turn the prison visiting room into the site of their "hot dates." I don't have that picture anymore, but I do have Michael's words describing, I think, the impression that Bree made on him. He shared the experience in the form of an essay that he had just written about "The Knight's Tale" and "The Miller's Tale" from Chaucer's *Canterbury Tales*. He called his essay "Two Tales and Four Desires."

In "The Knight's Tale," two cousins of royal blood have both been imprisoned for life in a tower. One of them, Palamon, glimpses a lady, Emily, walking in the garden near the prison. "Desire immediately sets in," Michael wrote and added, quoting Chaucer, "and Palamon wants Emily. He cries out in pain 'he blenched and gave a cry as though he had been stabbed, and to the heart.'" Like me, the cousin, Arcite, thinks Palamon's distress is caused by his imprisonment and chides him to endure. But "Palamon tells Arcite that prison has nothing to do with his distress but it is from a lady that he sees wandering in a garden below the tower." Arcite looks out the window "and he is also hurt by her beauty."

If "The Knight's Tale" tells the story of aristocrats in love, Michael wrote, "The Miller's Tale" tells a story of peasants in love, but a shared theme of desire's power unites the two tales. He concluded, "Desire is powerful and it creates a lot of other emotions. It makes men do things that they probably would not normally do." He expressed his core point this way: "In both tales, we could not predict the decisions that men filled by longing and desire would make. Nor could we correctly guess the outcome of their decisions."

Michael spoke oracular words. He prophesied. He knew, without knowing that he knew it, the course his life would take.

I was oblivious. I thought the essay was about Chaucer. No one could have guessed the final outcome of Michael's life because none of us took into account his most dizzying desire.

20.

THE BIGGEST WILDFIRE
IN CALIFORNIA HISTORY

All work and no play makes Jill a dull girl, but this has always been my way. As June heated up into July, and summer brought the threat of wildfire, I simply kept pushing Michael onward with his college courses. I cheered him on with his firefighting. Work and its rewards were what I could see then.

Now, I can see more. I believe that this year, 2003, was the best year of Michael's life. It was the year in which he learned how to drive. It was the year he wrote extraordinary things. It was also the year that he found love.

And it was the year he fought an inferno, the biggest wildfire in California history.

The California Fire Siege of 2003 burned some 800,000 acres. The largest single fire within it, the Cedar Fire, was and still is the biggest fire in California history, a blowup, shooting two hundred feet of flame in the sky. At one point, 80,000 acres incinerated in ten hours. Over two acres per second went up, in a raging roar like that of a fleet of freight trains, shatter-

FIRE BURNS ABOVE THE CITY OF SAN DIEGO

ing fields of crackling bones. Twenty-two people, including a firefighter, were burned or smoked to death.

Michael fought the Pass Fire, one of the first to burn. This 2,387-acre fire was reported at 4:11 P.M. on Tuesday, October 21, and raged through the dry grass and brush of Reche Canyon, north of Moreno Valley in Riverside County. Firefighters fought aggressively, battling exhaustion and heat across inaccessible terrain, cutting lines to forestall the fire's path, knowing the weathermen were predicting wind, holding the hot air in their lungs. The wind came and the fire jumped hither and yon, a broadjumper, a long jumper, now this way, now that, an erratic hurdler clearing the firefighters' lines. At its peak, it took 696 men, rapidly withering, parched, their legs turned to lead, to face down the fire. Three residences and two outbuildings were sacrificed, and then the gods were appeased.

Michael earned $1 a day fighting this fire. But that is not, of course, why he did it, and he never appeared to resent the wage. He did it because it was the most challenging, most meaningful, most rewarding thing he had ever had the chance to do. He recorded his experience in writing, a second tale of an inferno. Although he delivered it to me in a six-page single continuous paragraph printed single-spaced and in ALL CAPS, I've added paragraph breaks to make his fire report easier for you to read. In fighting fires, Michael found freedom.

Michael's Fire Narrative

On October 21, Tuesday, was the beginning of history. It was the beginning of the largest fire in the state of California. I'm a member of a CDF fire camp in Norco. We have a total of three hand crews that are trained in wildland fire fighting. The core of our training deals with the process of 'cutting line.' Cutting line is a process in which fuel is removed from the ground to the point of mineral soil or bare dirt. A full hand crew consists of a possible 19 men or women. 18 members are inmates and 1 member is the captain. On this particular day we had a crew of 13. We were working at the MWD (Metropolitan Water District) also known as Lake Mathews. On that day our captain was Shane Porter. The first call came in approximately at 12:30 or 1:00 p.m. The headquarters in Perris had dispatched a couple crews from Oakglen and Bautista. Oakglen and Bautista are also inmate CDF hand crews. The next couple of calls that came through were only for Oakglen and Bautista. Before the calls began coming in we

had a visual on what would turn out to be the Camp
Pendleton fire. As we work during that day we anticipated getting called to a fire. It began to seem that we
were not going to get called. As the day continued we
notice 3 more smoke columns; each in a different direction. We were almost certain that a call would come in
for one of Norco hand crews or even to dispatch our
strike team: 9382GULF. There are different types of
strike teams. When dealing with CDF hand crews, a
strike team is two hand crews coupled together as one
large hand crew. At 3:00, still no calls for Norco crews.
One of our captains makes a call on the radio in frustra-
tion, "Norco still does have fire crews." A couple of us
laughed because we understood and we as well were
becoming upset.

As the end of the day continued to approach we
had convinced ourselves that we were not going to get
called. I had spent most of the day hoping and waiting for a call. As we started to drive back to the camp,
myself and the crew had concluded that we did not
want to get called to the fire. We had resigned with
contentment just to go back to the facility to shower
and relax. One of the things that we were discussing on
the drive back was that the captain had said two of the
fires were federal and that they did not want any CDF
assistance. Apparently the fire that began in Fontana
was U.S. Forestry property. In my opinion that was a
lame excuse to refuse CDF assistance but from a political view I could see that they wanted to "milk the fire."
Meaning that they wanted the fire to continue burning

in order to make more money. With the help of CDF
hand crews the fire's progress is tremendously slowed.
When the fire is slowed down, it increases the contain-
ment. When the fire is being contained at a fast pace
it means the fire is almost out. I do not know whether
or not CDF hand crews were dispatched to that fire
but I do know that if multiple CDF hand crews were
dispatched on the same day when the fire began that
there could have been a significant decrease in what was
burned. Remember, I am only speculating but that does
not change the possibility that U.S. Forestry wanted
the fire to burn longer in order to make more money.
All of these things were discussed on our bus. When we
had arrived to the camp we had found out that Crew
1 and 3 had been dispatched to the Reche Canyon fire.
Myself and the other crew two members were glad that
it wasn't us. Additionally, out of our three crews, crew
two had the most fire hours which put us at the bottom
of the dispatched list. As we watch the other two crews
prepare to "strike it up," we stood around laughing
about how we were going to warm beds and T.V.s and
relaxing for the rest of the weekend. Of course that was
too good to be true. Several minutes later the captain
told crew two to Nomex up. We stared in disbelief
halfway hoping it was just a joke. I say halfway hoping
because in every single firefighter there is a switch of
adrenaline that is activated by the anticipation of being
on the fire line.

Before I continue I need to explain what it means to
Nomex up. All firefighters are required to wear Nomex

clothing (pants and shirt). Nomex is a fire resistant
material that protects the body from the heat of the fire.
Once we confirmed that it wasn't a joke we immediately got dressed in our Nomex and doubled checked
all of our safety gear. Crews one and three had left for
the Reche Canyon fire at about 4:45 or 5:00 p.m. My
crew didn't leave just yet because we had to wait for our
regular captain, Tony Hernandez. We waited anxiously
because from our camp we could see two separate fires
blackening the sky even before the darkness settled in.
We were all becoming hungry, and not wanting to go
on the mountain on an empty stomach, I passed out
two M.R.E.s (meals-ready-to-eat) to each crew man.
When the captain had finally arrived which was about
5:30 or 6:00 p.m. we were ready to go. After he had
arrived we still did not depart immediately. We left the
camp at approx. 7:00 o'clock. As we were driving down
the on-ramp of the freeway we could see the flames of
the Fontana fire. As we neared the Reche Canyon fire
we saw the flames were huge. Probably about 10 to 13
feet tall. In some other corners about 20 to 25 feet tall
because of the large amounts of fuel (grass, brush, trees,
etc.). When we had arrived we parked in what appeared
to be a temporary base or headquarters. There were
several engines, water tenders, and hand crews, all waiting for orders. When we had got there we saw Norco
crews 1 and 3, which is where we parked. We got off
the bus in full gear and waited for the captain to come
back to give us instructions. He told the crew that we
were waiting for further instructions. He told everyone

to check all of their safety gear again. To make sure that we all had our water and extra batteries stocked. He told the swamper and myself to carry fussees [flares] and flagging. We stayed for about 20 to 30 minutes until they told us to load up again. All of Norco's three hand crews drove to another location where we waited for maybe an hour and a half. The crew that I was a part of was still hungry. At that point I was laying next to the side of the bus resting. Another crew man passed out the M.R.E.s to the rest of the crew. The place that we were parked at was at the bottom of one of the many hills that was surrounding the area. We could see the fire burning but the anticipation had burned out. We had been working all day and now, tired from just driving around, we wanted to just sleep. I rested for only a little while before I got up to mingle with the other two crews. After waiting what seemed like hours we were told to load up again. We got on the freeway again and it seemed like we were driving in circles. I knew that we were driving to a location called the Pigeon Crest which I assumed was somewhere on the other side of the mountain. When we had got there, we did a hot tool out. A hot tool out is when the crew gets off the bus in hook line order (the order in which the crew is lined up and will work in). As each men gets off the bus he is handed his pre-assigned tool. I had to get off the bus first because I was responsible for passing out the hand tools. Once we were ready to go our captain gave us a safety briefing in which we ran through the ten fire standing orders and watch out situations. We then began hiking up a road that led to the side of a house. Once we reached the house we were on rocks and dirt with the fire blazing below us some 50 to 60 yards from us.

We started hiking several feet down the hill below the house. As we were going down the hill we passed by multiple cages that varied in the type of animals. There were goats, warthogs, sheep, rams, wolves, birds, and a few other types that I couldn't identify. We continued down this hill for a couple of feet and we turned upwards to cross over what seemed to be a huge piece of rock. We paused there for several seconds as our captain was receiving instructions. We stood there long enough for me to look down at the two other Norco crews as they had begun to engage in firefighting. I envied them because they were down there already and I smiled because for some it was their first time. I was a bit upset because I was at the back of the line. I was second in the lead and it was my responsibility to make sure that no one gets injured or falls behind. Each hand crew has a dragspoon and they are mandated to carry a first aid pack. So the captain is generally first and then the swamper, who is first in lead after the captain. I wanted to be in front in order to be where all the action was at. I had been on several fires by now, and it always seems like I miss out on the action. The captain, swamper, and dragspoon all carry shovels. My tool was a combination of a shovel and a rake at the end of a piece of heavy wood. The shovel is responsible for putting out flames with dirt. I have had to do a lot of shoveling on previous fires and expected not much on this particular fire.

The captain called out "tool out" which means to start
hiking.

"Tool" is stop hiking. We hiked over the rock that
was below the house and started hiking straight across
on the upper side of a hill. Because it was dark it was
very hard to see where we were walking. The path had
a lot of holes and slippery grass. And to make it worse,
it would take nothing but a mere slip to go falling down
the hill that was mined with rocks and rattle snakes.
We hiked maybe for about 20-30 yards across before
we started to go down. On hills like this one the path
could go down and then directly back up all while
going straight across. As we started to go down we had
to be careful because there were numerous drop offs.
The rocks were jagged and sometimes would go straight
down 7-8 feet and then going into another drop off
that was just as slippery and dangerous as the first. We
hiked down several of these and in the process one of
my crew tried to go around the drop on the bottom side
and slipped. I was unable to get to him immediately but
there had been a crew man from crew three that was
there to assist in coming down and he was able catch
him. At this point I thought about the Humboldt fire
when myself and two other crew men were sent back up
the mountain to get water and 600 feet of hose to bring
back down. The terrain in Humboldt was unforgiving
and mental error would have you falling back down
the mountain, possibly breaking bones or bashing one's
head on a rock. On the way back down one of my crew
men was maybe 30 feet in front of me. We were walk-

ing down the mountain backwards using the hose to
propel downwards. As I was holding the hose I heard
it bust below me. I stopped to turn around to see what
had happen. All I saw was my crew man tumbling down
what seems now had to have been a 80-90 feet drop.
I had let loose of the hose and started to immediately
slide down the mountain where it hard dropped off at. I
almost flew over the drop off and would have if I didn't
plant my left foot to a tree. When I had come to the
drop off, I asked him if he was o.k. He didn't respond
immediately but he was moving. I yelled to two other
firemen who I believe was from Station 62 or 61. They
told me to stay where I was and one of them went down
to get him. I was worried and fearful because I knew the
possibilities of being injured real bad. And it's disheart-
ening to see any firefighter get hurt real bad. I started
to feel guilty but I understood that there was nothing
that I could have done. We are trained to keep at least 10
feet between the man in front of you and going down
a steep hill more space is required in order to prevent
a domino effect of falls and cutting someone else with
your tool. Well, needless to say, he made it up o.k. yet,
on this Reche Fire, after that slip I became 100 percent
more aware and alert.

　　We all made it down safely and joined the other two
crews. Our crew had to go back some yards and start
cutting line where the fire had already ceased burning. When we caught up to the other two crews almost
everyone was working. Some were just standing and
watching. At that point all of the shovels were called

to the front. When I had got up to the front the flames were high and hot. I could feel myself growing stronger instantly. My captain had told me and the swamper to stay in front to throw dirt on the fire. Immediately I was working. I surveyed the line of the fire and its approach. Myself and a couple of other shovels formed a line started to throw dirt on the fire. Sometimes I was 3 to 4 feet from the fire and at other times I was two feet away. The shovels dictated which way the line would be cut. We followed along the length of the fire working hard. The other two crews had given a couple of shovels to some of the other crew man. Crew men would switch when tired. At one point a crew man was standing in the way and I had to scream at him 'if you're tired, get the hell out of the way. You're slowing everybody else down.' He accepted what I said because I was a known worker. Although I had only been on the crew for three months I was a quick learner. I had established myself as a person who wanted and enjoyed getting the job. As I worked I could feel my arms and shoulders become as heavy as mortar stones. But that only fueled me. While we worked, the three crews began to merge as one.

Some way or another I ended up being the front shovel. When you're working in the fire line your only concern is doing the job and you can work so hard that when you look up you will see several differences. In this instance that I looked up I noticed that I was in front. I also noticed that we had covered a lot of ground. I tried to take a fresh and deep breath but that was unsuccessful. Most of the time when you're up

FIRE BURNS ALONG A HILL LINE ENDANGERING HOMES

front it is plague with smoke that waters your eyes. Our
captain has this example of what it is to fight fire. He
says that if you haven't been at a fire where you are constantly tearing up, breathing hard, and drinking your
own snot, then you haven't fought a fire. Forgive me
for what may appear disgusting but for every firefighter
these aspects are as real as death.

If you haven't been put in a position to when you
have to run from the fire, it is for two reasons. The
first is because you were safe and the second is because
you were blessed. Even when enforcing the safety rules
and watch out situations, anything can happen. What
seems safe one minute, can mean death in the next
second. Mere change in the direction of the wind can

have you running from a fire that more than likely is
burning faster than you are running. That is why it is
very important to stay aware of what is going on. For a
second I didn't, and that could have been costly. I had to
turn around for a second to find some fresh air before I
continued. Once I had gathered myself, I observed what
the fire was doing. I looked back to see the saws really
going at it. Some underestimate the work of using a saw
during a fire which is why many don't last on the saw.
To use the saw takes strength, determination, and heart.
It is a very grueling task and probably the most important one. The crew man using the saw has to cut brush,
trees, and it is difficult to do in the night on slippery
grass and rocky drop offs. I must admire the resiliency
needed in saw men to get the job done. When I turned
around I saw that the path we were going on was going
to drop off in trees and thick brush that seems to stand
like brick walls. I went back to shoveling dirt onto
the fire and for several yards ahead I could see that the
flames weren't as high as when we had first begun. My
swamper had radioed the captain to see if there were any
further instructions or should we change our approach.

The captain responded to continue in the direction that we were going. The swamper started down
a steep and thick brushed dropoff. I followed behind
him. The saws were maybe ten to fifteen feet behind us.
Once we got down the drop off it became difficult to
determine which way to go. The fire had burned out
in this particular drop off, so there was no heat to deal
with except what rested within the ground. There were

hundreds of branches, as thick as Louisville Bats, going every single direction, up and down, left and right. The swamper had to use his shovel to break up certain parts of the brush and when he couldn't maneuver his tool he would have to use feet and legs to break the restraining brush. The captain radioed him to come back for some reason or another. It left me up front to make a path for the saws. I had to follow along the burn so that nothing would be missed. It was very dark and although we had head lamps, the brush was so thick you couldn't really see which direction was best. I heard the saws coming down behind me as they were cutting line. At that point, as I was working through the brush, my pack and nomex got caught on some branches. As I tried to untangle myself I became frustrated because the branches would break. Why? I have no idea. I slipped on a thicket. I hadn't realized how tired I was until I was trying to get out. . . . It seemed like it took forever to get out and I was physically exhausted but that meant very little too me. Although spending quite a bit of energy in untangling myself, I managed to get a second wind. . . . I continued to guide the saws through the brush. Of course, it would be easier for them to get through because they had a machine to cut the brush but that doesn't include fatigue and being just tired. We had strong saws that I had cut through thick brush and probably on much worse terrain. I guided them for maybe 40 to 50 minutes before we came around one of the mountains on which the fire was burning on.

When I came around, after crawling through and

under the brush, I was greeted with another part of the fire that was burning crazy. The danger was that there were several trees burning that were 35 to 40 feet tall. As I got closer to get a better look at the area, I saw a tree that was maybe 60 feet tall that was burning in and out of the tree. The branches on top of the tree were burning as much and at intervals were falling down. The saws were about 30 feet behind me. I saw a few of the captains on top of the hill so I hiked up real fast to explain to them the situation and the terrain. My captain told me to go back down to where the saws were and to bring them up and away from the burning trees. We took a small break because for an unknown reason nothing else around the trees was burning. We waited for the tree to burn out so we could cut line on the green side of it. It took about 30 minutes before the tree was burned out. There was still a tremendous danger because the tree was still burning within and at any time it could fall over.

One of the swampers flagged the tree with flagging that says, "Killer Tree." I'm not sure which one did it but afterwards we all got back up and went down the hill back into the drop off. It was easier going up then it was going down. We formed a super crew between the three crews and went back at it. It was approximately 1:00 o'clock in the morning. Once we were past the burning tree, the terrain became easier. We continued to cut line for about 20 minutes and the burn started to turn upwards at a curve going up a steep hill. We had been cutting line without any fire near for several

minutes but as we started up, we could see the fire on
the hill. It was burning fast. It was pitch dark except for
the light was emanating from the flames. When we were
on top of the hill waiting for the tree to burn out, you
could see engines because their lights were on but down
in the drop you could see nothing. The only light that
existed was what was given by the head lamp. When the
captains saw the fire on the hill, they immediately called
the shovels to go up the hill first. Myself and two other
swampers went up immediately. The other guys who
were assigned shovels had managed to hide. I'm assum-
ing that they were tired and I mention that for several of
these guys this was their first fire.

As we climbed up the hill, as fast we could, we could
see that the fuel on the hill was thick and tall. Once we
got up there we started shoveling dirt onto the flames.
Captain John Harrell was right up there with us shoveling dirt onto the fire. Captain Harrell was old, very old,
but you wouldn't know of it, unless you were told so.
He had the most hike out of all the captains. He stood
about 5'4" and probably weighed about 165lbs. You
rarely find captains that are willing to work and be on
the front line where the fire is at. I respect him a lot
because he was always working and he had a love for
the job and it wasn't just work for him. Since the brush
was so thick, the smoke as well was very thick and the
shrouds that we are given as a part of safety gear aren't
always enough to protect from inhalation. . . . As we
worked deeper into the burning area, there were constantly multiple drop-offs. I must remind you that it was

very dark. At this point the light that we were receiving
was from the fire.

Once we completed that task we hiked up to where
the other two crews had stopped at to rest. We got there
and took our gear off and rested for about an hour. That
was when they had delivered lunch to us or breakfast. I
think it was about four in the morning. . . . The captain
called us into a circle and gave us the instructions for
our next assignment. We were to protect three houses
while U.S. Forestry back burned a particular hillside
even though the area that was being burned was about
a football field away. Whoever's decision it was felt it
necessary to have hand crew near more or less. It was
for show. After being on your feet all night we would
rather be fighting fire instead of standing on guard.
What was more insulting was the fact that there were
a few engines that were there. These engines can stop
a fire faster than a hand crew. I'm not quite sure what
was the reason for us being there. We stood between
the back burning area and the homes about twenty to
thirty feet apart. I was able to nap during intervals while
standing. The only thing I do better than firefighting is
sleeping. One of the battalion chiefs pulled up to talk
to our captain. Apparently, they knew each other based
on them hugging and shaking hands. When you have
been fighting fires for a long time, you accumulate a lot
of acquaintances. After they talked for about twenty
minutes, the captain said that we could sit down but we
had to keep our gear on, including helmets.

———

HERE ENDS MICHAEL'S REPORT on the Pass Fire and the California Fire Siege of 2003.

In the days after Michael's experience fighting the Pass Fire, we talked about it a lot on the phone. I was hugely moved by his experience, by the matter-of-fact way that he described fires I'd seen in photos and that even just as images struck terror in my heart. I couldn't imagine the intensity of the heat. I urged Michael to write up his story. He committed to a daily writing goal, promising to send me his memoir at the end of the week. The ALL CAPS 6-page continuous paragraph that he mailed captured the unrelenting attention a firefighter must give to fire. You can't change direction, you can't break your glance, you must know where the fire is, you must keep moving without cease. In the heat, you can barely take a breath. You must never let your guard down, ever.

The more formal 99-page after-disaster report on the October Fire Siege mentions inmate crews twice, once in a small photo and once in the final section of recommendations: "IT IS FURTHER ORDERED that the California Department of Corrections and the California Youth Authority place the highest priority for assignment of level one inmates and wards to staff Conservation Camp Fire Crews." Although the Department of Forestry wanted as many invisible firemen as it could get its hands on, the inmate crews didn't get any ticker-tape parades or keys to the city. The members of these crews knew, though, that they were doing worthy work. Michael's words attest to that.

I'm convinced that Michael became the man he believed

he could be when he was on the line, the lead shovel, slowing down a fire's path. The heat and screaming crackle of fire brought focus, too, to his academic efforts. In his college course during this period, he also became the man he believed he could be and finally completed a course. The outdoor time helped concentrate the indoor time.

In the year of the Fire Siege, Michael found the secret to his well-being: fires, books, and love. He was one of the lucky ones. Not yet among the millions lost, he had, if fleetingly, found himself.

YET MICHAEL'S PLEASURES ON sweaty days of training and hot and smoky days of firefighting weren't altogether pure.

In the years since his death, I've discovered many things about Michael that I didn't know. Some are harder to take than others. Here's one of the toughest. Sometime in this period, Michael the valiant firefighter also began ferrying drugs into prison in his anus. Perhaps that's why the $1-per-day wage didn't bother him.

Other things, too, mean that this period of light also held darkness. In May 2004, unrest in the prison culminated in the death of an inmate and an especially long lockdown. Michael never told me about this death and lockdown; I learned about it from inmate family chat sites. On the whole, he kept such darkness to himself.

This pattern of reserve broke a year after the Pass Fire when Michael had some sort of personal crisis—I imagine having to do with Bree. One of the features of communicating with an inmate is that the conversation—whether on the phone, visiting, or in writing—is never fulsome. All talk is recorded or under surveillance; letters are opened and invariably reviewed. Consequently, much goes unsaid or only obliquely expressed, as if in code. This is why I can only imagine what the cause might have been of the single most despairing letter I ever got from him. In a missive dated to October 2004, the darkness, whatever its source, broke through:

> I'm tired and worn out. Everything is becoming more harder to deal with. I'm not writing this seeking comfort but I'm not sure why I'm writing this. . . . Danielle, I'm holding on for dear life and it seems like I'm losing grips on everything. I cry uncontrollably at night. There are few good days and moments that are painful seem to last forever. I stay up late to avoid reflection when I lay down. I do as much as possible during the day to tire myself out so I can sleep through the night. I'll finish this some other time. Love always, Michael.

This, I think, was lovelorn Michael. None of Michael's family or friends ever knew him to use drugs. He didn't receive any medical attention during this period, so he wasn't ill. Something had gone awry, I believe, with the first love of his life. But because so much was communicated obliquely in all of our conversations and our correspondence, I can only speculate. This letter makes clear, though, that the darkness could be deep. Against this backdrop, the light of the year of the Fire Siege shines out all the brighter.

As I have assembled the fragmentary shards of what my family members know about Michael's prison time, the most powerful thing to have jumped out is the surprising discovery that he can indeed be said to have had one very good year.

The year of the Fire Siege was the high point of Michael's life.

His letters, his essays, his fire memoir, all seem to sing, to proclaim a yearlong chorus of hosannas. This was the period when—hot off his *Inferno* essay, on the cusp of learning what it is to fight fire—he wrote, "Several years ago all I could see was a hill of years to climb. I've made it up top and now I'm running down."

Only in that year could he write, "Time is flying by so fast I can hardly keep up with the days."

III

UNFORGIVING WORLD

Some say the world
will end in fire,
Some say in ice.

—ROBERT FROST

21.

FIRE AND ICE

Bree came from a world where cousins, or at least one of her cousins, could call hits. Yet Michael loved Bree permanently. Their love was, as he would say, "Love always." This love anchored him to the world of these other cousins, and their guns and drugs. When asked to choose, he affirmed his love of Bree.

This is why he died.

Why did Michael love Bree? He loved her because she was the most beautiful woman he had seen as he came of age with heterosexual desires inside an all-male prison. Who knows when Michael was first sodomized. Probably it was when he was first transferred to adult prison in Susanville and, in Centinela the older inmates, the lifers, as he put it, "took care of him." But Michael and Bree were age mates. Out of all the men in prison she could have had, she chose him. His family loved him, and he loved his family, because he was born to them. He and Bree chose one another in a world with little room for choice, a gift to one another of surpassing value.

But why was Michael in prison long enough to meet and fall in love so inextricably with someone who, in the end, was plainly bad for him? Why did he have to pass from boy to man, an odyssey of eleven years, behind bars?

By the time Michael, as a teenager, was punished in 1995, California legislators had given up on rehabilitation in prison. They had given up on rehabilitation even for juveniles. Critics of the penal system say that all the time. Here is what they don't say. Legislators had also given up on retribution, the idea that the punishment should fit the crime. Retribution actually puts a limit on how much punishment you can impose. The California Assembly members who voted unanimously to try as adults sixteen-year-olds, and then fourteen-year-olds, for carjacking had all become deterrence theorists. They were designing sentences not for people but for a thing: the aggregate level of crime. They wanted to reduce the totality of crime; they didn't have any interest in justice for any individual person, whether victim or perpetrator. The target of Michael's sentence was not Michael, a fifteen-year-old boy with a bright mind and a mild proclivity, as we shall see, for theft, but the 2,663 carjackings that occurred in Los Angeles between January and August of 1993. I don't know how high that number was by the time Michael stood before the judge in the spring of 1995, but Michael stood in, in essence, for all of those jackings, just as did every other defendant who passed before the bench. Deterrence dehumanizes. It directs at the individual the full hate that society understandably bears toward an aggregate phenomenon. But no individual can or should bear that kind of responsibility. Such an approach to punishment is unconscionable. The concept of "just deserts" is meant to protect people from excess.

Since antiquity, mankind has known that anger drives retribution, the desire to make someone pay. When punishment fits the crime, anger sates itself; it modulates; it softens. This is what makes it anger, not hatred, a distinction recognized by philosophers all the way back in antiquity. Hatred is distinguished by its unending quality, its rigid fixity and imperviousness to softening. A proposed punishment for a fifteen-year-old of twenty-five years to life for a first arrest after a freely confessed week's crime spree and failed carjacking in all of which that fifteen-year-old was the only person physically injured is one of the purest expressions of hatred I can imagine. The economists Claudia Goldin and Larry Katz sing the praises of an American educational system that generated opportunity in this country for two centuries because it was a "forgiving or second-chance" system. But our world is forgiving no longer. Michael was in prison for eleven years from adolescent bloom to full manhood, long enough to form a life-altering bond to a fellow inmate, because we have built an unforgiving world.

So we lost my baby cousin when he was twenty-nine. Why, cuz? Cuz of fire; cuz of ice. In his poem, "Fire and Ice," Robert Frost condenses the whole of Dante's *Inferno* into nine lines.

> *Some say the world will end in fire,*
> *Some say in ice.*
> *From what I've tasted of desire*
> *I hold with those who favor fire.*

> *But if it had to perish twice,*
> *I think I know enough of hate*
> *To say that for destruction ice*
> *Is also great*
> *And would suffice.*

Society's hatred of rising violence served up a disproportionate sentence for Michael. His own desire for Bree tethered him to a violent world. Ice and fire. Fire and ice. Both brought him to his destruction.

Yet the why's don't end there, nor do the reasons. The deepest question remains. How exactly did fifteen-year-old Michael come to be holding a gun in a Southern California carport on a foggy Sunday morning in September 1995 intending to separate a man from his possessions? Was it fire? Or was it ice?

22.

THE SINGLE MOTHER AND
THE GREAT WHITE WHALE

Michael Alexander Allen was born on November 30, 1979, sole survivor of a twin conception, to a twenty-three-year old single mother who lived with her sister, Roslyn, and her sister's lover, Brenda. Two older siblings also welcomed him into the world.

Michael had such a huge head when he was born that the doctor thought there was water on his brain. But he came out smiling and laughing and so was introduced to the family as the baby with personality and charisma. This was a baby we all wanted to cuddle.

His mother, Karen, hadn't been a single mother for long. Just the previous summer, she had left the father of her three children, whom she had met the summer after her junior year in high school in Fernandina Beach, Florida, where she was born, a little fishing village on Amelia Island, the southernmost of the Sea Islands running along the Atlantic Coast. Karen was the baby daughter of a fishing boat captain and his

NEWBORN

second wife, a midwife and informal community nurse. Karen was twelfth in a big brood; seventh to this mother. During the decade of the 1950s, African Americans entered the professional workforce in dramatic numbers. The number of black nurses in the country doubled from 3,500 to nearly 7,000. Karen's mother didn't have a degree, but she was among those serving her community as a nurse. This was a family with grit.

Karen fell in love the summer after her junior year in high school. Paul Johnson was the lucky man, a construction worker, who was working on all the new condominiums springing up that would transform Amelia Island into a posh resort. He popped diet pills and took speed, and, to Karen, represented money, fancy cars, and drugs. She herself drank a little and smoked weed. Although cocaine was flowing into

Florida in the 1970s, PCP was as fancy as it got with Paul. He was also married.

During Karen's freshman year in college, in 1975, she dropped out at the start of the spring semester, started working at a bus station and later a nursing home. Then she moved in with Paul. Their first child, Nicholas, was born in November. Karen didn't drink or smoke while she was pregnant because smoking made her feel nauseous. That was how she always first realized that she was pregnant, the fact that the weed made her feel sick. In November 1977, Paul and Karen's second child, a daughter, Roslyn, was born, a quiet personality like her older brother who would grow up to be as big-hearted as her mother.

By the time that Karen was again pregnant, things had turned hard with Paul. He had consistently told her that he and his wife were divorcing but this never happened. Then, Karen learned that Paul and his so-called wife weren't married after all. There had never been any legal impediment to their marrying, if Paul had only wanted to. This startled Karen into self-awareness. School was also deepening her self-confidence. Following in the footsteps of her mother, she was even preparing to start nursing school. Her sister Roslyn had promised to pay for it. Karen had a desire for education, and with Paul she also began "requesting and moving with more freedom." The result was that "his jealousy just became incredible."

Paul became "abusive, surprisingly"—surprisingly physically abusive. He accused her of infidelity, charging that this third pregnancy, this being Michael, was not his child. He pinched baby Roslyn. He beat Karen. "The first time he beat me, my face was unrecognizable. I tried to go to work,"

Karen recalls, but her coworkers sent her home. On one occasion when Paul went after Roslyn, Karen got a knife. "That moment I found some strength within me and I said this is not going to keep going. I wanted to fight." Paul tried to choke her. Somehow they resolved that altercation without injury, and thereafter they managed to avoid such severe physical fights, but the conflict didn't stop. Karen began to express herself more vocally but also to play little tricks on him.

"I would bake sweet potato pies and I wouldn't eat it, and he was thinking I was trying to poison him. That's the kind of stuff I did." There was a voice that was waking up inside her.

In her second trimester with Michael, Karen flew to Southern California to visit siblings who in the late 1960s and early 1970s had moved there, like so many other African Americans seeking opportunity outside the Deep South. This visit permitted an opportunity for conversation, especially with her sister and her sister's girlfriend, and conversation brought clarity. She settled her mind on moving away from Paul and to Los Angeles. During her visit, she started to organize welfare, medical benefits, and food stamps. Returning to Florida, she packed impractically—books, tennis rackets, and dishes—and left, taking Nicholas and Roslyn. She says that if the violence hadn't been there with Paul, she would be there still, living with Paul in tropical coastal Florida. She was committed to the idea of family. But instead Nestor Avenue in Carson, California, Big Roslyn's house, was home when Michael was born.

23.

FIRST STEPS

Michael's aunt, Big Ros, who gave him his first home, wanted to make sure that her little sister, Karen, would get up on her own two feet. From the get-go, she told Karen she wouldn't be able to stay; she shouldn't get comfortable. Two months into the Iran hostage crisis, a month after Michael's birth, and just after Christmas, Big Ros made good on her promise to evict the family and sent them packing to live with another sibling, their brother Daniel. The plan was for Karen to stay there until she found a job.

The 1979 oil crisis had sent the economy shuddering into a recession with interminably long lines at gas stations. Although African American unemployment would soon reach historical highs, within a month Karen found a job as a certified nursing assistant. In following in the footsteps of her mother, a nurse, she had lucked into work in one of the few growth areas of the economy, service jobs in the health industry. This would permit her to inch her way forward in the years to come.

FIRST STEPS

But good fortune was cut with bad. This country girl from northern Florida with the overbite and sweet smile could not possibly have guessed back then in 1979 that another service industry was growing just as fast as her own. She could not have guessed that Los Angeles was poised to become the largest urban market within the world's largest market for illegal narcotics. The United States is and has for some time been the world's single biggest importer of illegal drugs. Our shifting tastes for heroin, marijuana, and cocaine make and break fortunes the world over. Hardly a late-twentieth-century development, this has been true since 1933 when the first Prohibition, against alcohol, ended, and the Mafia found a substitute product in heroin.

It needs to be known that La Cosa Nostra built its heroin

business first in New York, in Harlem. The black community there was, sadly, an easy mark. Proximate to La Cosa Nostra's own East Harlem neighborhood, Harlem in the post-Depression 1940s was full of people on the skids ripe for recruitment into addiction. There were small-scale black criminal groups, though nothing like the Mafia's own level of organized crime. But these groups were ready to pick up street-level distribution. The powers-that-be, whether in police or politics, were unlikely to be too troubled by the further degradation of the African American community. An East Harlem Italian mob neighborhood became the epicenter for distribution, and by the end of the 1940s, addiction had already become entrenched in Harlem's African American community. Bellevue Hospital in New York saw six youth admitted for heroin in 1950, then seventy-four in the first sixth months of 1951. Fifty-two of these were black.

The powers-that-be, as it were, got bothered only later, especially when drug use spread to the troops in Vietnam. Everyone noticed when Richard Nixon launched the War on Drugs in 1971, and the 1973 Rockefeller drug laws criminalized not only trafficking but also possession, and outlawed not only heroin and cocaine but also marijuana. What few people could have known in 1979, when Karen decided to venture west to Los Angeles, was that one of Nixon's first moves, that of shutting down the Mafia's French Connection, had the effect of busting the American narcotics market wide open, which afforded opportunity for entry to traffickers from Colombia, Mexico, and Southeast Asia. Globalization was about to arrive, destination, Los Angeles.

As Barbara Streisand crooned "No More Tears," and people played and replayed Marvin Gaye's "What's Going On," there was simply no way for Karen to know that a plague of violence was about to break out throughout the Southland. The country girl from northern Florida, still so unvarnished, saw only opportunity in the City of Angels.

24.

"SIS, RUN!"

When Karen got her first certified nursing assistant job, she moved her young family to Normandie and 104th near Southwest Community College in Watts, a small quadrant of that Los Angeles neighborhood that, in fact, had had no looting, arson, or damage during the Watts riots fifteen years earlier. Michael was too young to remember the difficulty of his family's first sojourn in a home of their own, as his mother woke him and his older brother and sister at 4 A.M. so that they could head to the babysitter on an exhaust-belching city bus, before Karen turned around and headed to a workplace that she didn't reach until 7:15 A.M. To help South Los Angeles, bus fares had been reduced to 50 cents for three years, and Michael and his family joined waves of Angelenos who helped public transit in Los Angeles reach its modern peak in ridership.

Then at the end of the day, they reversed the trip. Karen recalls, "By the time we got home, and I bathed and fed the kids and then ate, drank, and passed out, it was time to do it all over again." Michael wouldn't have remembered his mother's descent into drink in the months following his birth, but by July of 1980, she needed Alcoholics Anonymous. It was a quick descent but a dramatic and durable reversal. She has been sober since before Michael turned one.

At this point, Karen started a slow, hard-fought upward climb. In the year after she started AA, she got a new job, once again as a certified nursing assistant, this time at Harbor-UCLA Medical Center, where Michael had been born and where he would later be hospitalized for his gunshot wound. She graduated from the buses and acquired a little, used blue Datsun. She moved her family up to a little more space, at 103rd and Wilmington. The neighborhood had been one of the worst flashpoints during the civil unrest of 1965. Two people had died just down the street. When the local grocery store reopened, only women were allowed inside. But the neighborhood was also just around the corner from the Watts Towers, where there were art classes for children, and it had been a center of intellectual and artistic activism in the sixties and seventies.

To make getting a bigger place possible, Karen took on roommates. She also thought of the roommates as potential babysitters. "That was always the thing, trying to find childcare," she recalls. She was always trying to make all the pieces fit, without quite enough material resources to make it happen, like trying to button a sweater over a pregnant belly. She remembers being struck, once, when someone asked her why she tried so hard when it was obvious she didn't have the resources to hold it all together. She'd never stopped long enough to think about it, she realized.

Of course, the roommates, friends of friends or even near

strangers, also brought complications. With one roommate, a gay man, she finally discovered that "he was having company while I was working, when he was supposed to be looking after the kids." Yet Karen's kids always had a place to sleep, clothes, at least one pair of shoes; and they never went hungry. When she had to, she would get her hands on food stamps, even if she had to lie.

Michael probably would have remembered this second home, where the family moved when he was about two. He always wanted to be outdoors and so would have remembered the neighborhood around it. He enjoyed the preschool in the apartment complex, tumbling about in shorts that showed his chubby thighs, even when it was cool enough that all the other kids wore pants. He would have remembered baking with his mom, and Thanksgivings and Christmases with all his uncles, aunts, and cousins.

This was how Karen's kids got extras—holiday presents from family members. If Michael got toy cars, or a tricycle, or action figurines and Legos, it was usually because the extended family had piled up the Christmas tree at someone's house and Karen and the kids came along. Together, over holidays, the group of California cousins that included Karen's kids, my brother and me, and several other sets of cousins, all learned to eat giblets and sweet potato pie.

Sometimes J. P. and his third wife, Grace, even flew out from Florida, and J. P. would dress in the regal garb of an African prince for particularly special occasions. Inevitably, there were footraces in the street and football games on a front lawn, and college football on TV. Thanks to these gatherings, Karen never had to worry about laying in presents for her brood. She

CHILDHOOD

could count on Big Ros and her brothers to do that, while she focused on a roof, food, shoes.

Yet even with this kind of support from family, parenting three young kids while working full-time was too much for Karen. In the early 1980s, she sent Roslyn for a couple of years to live with Big Ros. The result was that Roslyn felt her mother didn't love her while Michael and Nicholas believed that, since she'd sent Roslyn some place nicer, she loved Roslyn more. Sometime in those years, when Michael was about four or five, a friend of his mother's, Babi Tunde, taught him to meditate. This would become a lifelong practice, the only way he had to be still. From Michael's early years, his mother would sometimes find him on the roof meditating.

Despite the emotional drama among the siblings, the downsizing was worth it. With this little bit of breathing room, Karen was finally able to start nursing school and head toward realizing her mother's dreams. She enrolled in 1983 and graduated in 1984, when her three kids were eight, six, and four. I remember the barebones graduation ceremony, held in the gym of an area high school, rows of family on folding chairs as a group of mostly women walked across the stage. Now in seventh grade, I was proud of my aunt. Her struggles had been a constant refrain in my childhood, a basic harmony against which we lived out our lives as a family. Sometimes her phone was on; sometimes it was off. This month there was a bill she needed a little help with. Every now and then the electricity went off. When she hauled herself over the finish line of that nursing degree, I was as puffed up with pride as anyone in that little auditorium. I knew it had taken her a steel will to get there.

And that degree made a huge difference. Karen was able to step up to jobs at the next level. In 1986, when a friend's cigarettes set fire to their apartment at 103rd and Wilmington, she was able to move her family not just into another apartment in Watts but out of Watts into a rented house in Highland Park, just southeast of Pasadena. Instead of treeless streets lined by walk-up apartment buildings, rows of bungalows defined this neighborhood, and there was plenty of grass and trees. This was the place the kids called home. They had decent schools. The neighborhood was multiethnic and the kids made friends up and down the street.

Karen and the kids lived in a house, a little dark brown three-bedroom California cottage, with a crawl space beneath it. Now Michael didn't just wander up to the roof to meditate but also into the crawl space. Or he climbed the trees outside.

 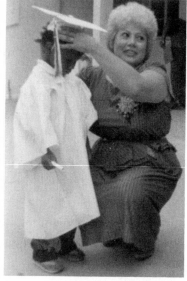

KINDERGARTEN GRADUATION

He made a lot of friends. Robin, Pauline, and Francis. Robert who lived next door. The kids in the anti-abortion family across the street.

And then he ventured out upon a boy's adventures. Playing with matches one day, he set fire to a rug in a neighbor's house, and he tormented his sister by playing with electrical cords. He cut the TV cord in order to show her a magic trick. He would show her how he could turn the TV on and off by re-connecting or separating the two ends of the cut cord. When he did bad, and sometimes even when he hadn't but when his mother thought he had, she would smack him. On the head, the legs, the arms.

So there were difficulties, but good things, too.

In Highland Park, the rites of passage proceeded according to plan. Michael's beautiful kindergarten teacher, the one with the blond Afro, loved him. He graduated in high style in a white cap and gown. He had gymnastic lessons and played Little League and went to summer camp. To raise the funds for camp, he sold peanuts, so successfully even that he funded his brother and sister's trips to camp, too. The trio would go for three-week stints in the summer. Then they would come home. Their mother would do their laundry, and then she would send them off again. They always went together.

Michael also had a glorious bicycle, a He-Man bike, that he loved, and their house was on top of a hill. He would fly down it barefoot, not yet able to brake, ending up at least once with a swollen eye with the bike all bent out of shape, having terrified his sister, cousins, mother, anyone who was around.

His sister, who was growing into a large-bodied girl and had already developed a mothering instinct, would cry out,

MICHAEL ON THE HILLSIDE SIDEWALK WHERE HE
CRASHED HIS BIKE

"Michael, why don't you put no shoes on!" We visited them
often at this house. Once a month from sixth to eighth grade,
I would come by so Big Ros's girlfriend could relax my hair.

The only slightly unusual ritual in Michael's life at the time
was Ala-Tots. Since he couldn't have remembered his mother's
drinking, his enrollment in the program must have seemed
mysterious. Karen's spirit lightens when she talks about their
time in Highland Park and how amusing it was to eavesdrop
on the kids' Saturday morning Ala-Tot meetings. The trio
would gather outside her bedroom door, whispering up a
cloud of buzzing bees. They were whispering out their griev-
ances which, she presumed, were mainly about her. They were

a united front, and in this small house all four of them had five years they are glad to remember.

These same years were bad ones, though, for the City of Angels. No one can precisely date the invention of crack cocaine, but call it 1979 or 1980. It was around then. This highly addictive poor man's version of the rich man's high brought an upswing both in addiction and in the violence that went along with illegal trafficking. The onset of the crack epidemic is generally dated to 1983, the year that Karen entered nursing school. With its arrival, the intertwining of street gangs and drug traffickers accelerated, a deadly double helix. Between 1983 and 1985, cocaine sales involving gang members increased from 9 percent to 25 percent of the total traffic. In other words, gangs in the early eighties did not dominate the L.A. cocaine market, but their degree of involvement would increase throughout the decade. To the degree that street gangs did participate in the drug business, they brought younger participants and more African Americans into the game. Along with the new link between the drug business and gangs came a surge in gang-related violence. In Los Angeles, "the [annual] number of gang related homicides went from 212 in 1983 to 800 by 1992." The drug business fueled a transformation of gangs that had once been mainly about juvenile delinquency into something far more violent.

Karen moved her family to Highland Park because she thought it was safer than Los Angeles, but by 1983, the invisible world beneath Los Angeles' surface, where you "either jacked for money or you sold dope" and where "working was considered weak," had begun to seep eastward. "Revenue," as it was called, was changing the landscape of the gangs.

Roslyn remembers walking to church one Sunday when a group of boys with crowbars jumped out of a car and ran toward them. "Sis, run!" her brother, Nicholas, shouted as he dove under a car to hide. Roslyn ran all the way to church.

This is how Karen and Roslyn learned that Nicholas, now thirteen, had started gangbanging in Highland Park.

25.

GANGBANGING—
A DEFINITION

What does it mean to gangbang? What did it mean in 1988, when Nicholas started? Here's the current definition from urbandictionary.com: "to be posted on yo set or turf and protect it or sell drugs on it." But gangbanging didn't always mean selling drugs. Once upon a time all it meant was protecting turf.

The story about gangs reaches way back. Give me a little bit of space to profess.

In the early twentieth century, waves of African Americans migrated from the rural South to the urban North, the exodus resulting in massively overcrowded black slums in many cities, not only in New York but also Chicago and Philadelphia. Suddenly, the North in many ways took on the hue of the South. The professed liberalism of the pre–Civil War North frayed in the presence of refugees from the lynching epidemic below the Mason-Dixon line. With restrictive covenants and spasmodic violence, preexisting and defensive white populations, who themselves were a multiethnic stew in the wake of late-nineteenth-century immigration, sought to limit the "territory" the newcomers might "invade." Not only street actions but also the official policy vocabulary of the period borrowed from the language of pest control. In addition to confronting residential segregation, African Americans all too often also encountered blatant discrimination. Jobs were harder to come by than anticipated, and for African Americans in particular, the Great Depression eradicated the small gains of the preceding decades. In the 1940s, African Americans were wedged together in overcrowded pockets of places like New York, Philadelphia, Chicago, and Los Angeles—and they were out of work.

The situation in the early twentieth century was similar in the Southwest. Large numbers of Mexicans migrated into Texas, Arizona, and California, joining Mexican American populations who had been on that land already for generations, even before the United States annexed these territories from Mexico in 1845. They, too, were confronted with segregation and discrimination. And during the Depression, this country deported more than 12,000 people of Mexican descent, including American citizens, further poisoning relationships between Mexican Americans and whites.

Given the intense competition over land and labor, white-on-black race riots flared between 1917 and 1923 in East St. Louis; Chester, Pennsylvania; Philadelphia; Houston; Washington D.C.; Chicago; Omaha; Charleston, South Carolina; Longview, Texas; Knoxville; Elaine, Arkansas; West Frankfort, Illinois; Rosewood, Florida; and, famously, Tulsa. In the wake of the Depression, Harlem experienced its own cycle of race riots, in both 1935 and 1943. And also in 1943, on the West Coast, Los Angeles witnessed the so-called "Zoot Suit Riots," when U.S. sailors and marines attacked Latino youths. Further domino effect riots against Latinos spread to Chicago, San Diego, Oakland, Evansville, Philadelphia, and New York.

America's story in the twentieth century is in so many ways a sordid tale. It is the story, a tragic litany, of the things people have done to survive in a rapaciously competitive, ethnically and racially fractured society. White racism is a part of this story but, mind you, only a part. Pretty much everybody was out for his or her own and lined up against everybody else. Across the country, gangs formed as "self-protection" societies in response to harassment from larger ethnic groups. The harassment could fly in all kinds of directions, and as gangs emerged, they could also brew rivalries within the ethnic group from which they came. Exhibit A is the Mafia and its feuding families.

One oral history tells a story this way about how, in the 1930s, "The leaders of the [Catholic] Church [in Los Angeles] sponsored an athletic club to foster brotherhood and friendship among the Mexican/Chicano minority members within the community." The Church was responding to the emergence of gangs in the previous decade, and trying to channel the social energies in a positive direction. Because there had been "a lot of racism and violence towards Chicanos and Mexican immigrants in the Boyle Heights area," and because "school aged children were regularly harassed and bullied by members of the larger ethnic groups," the boys in the community "decided to form a self-protection group which would serve as escorts to and from school for their younger brothers and sisters." They called themselves "White Fence." As they grew, they began to war with other Chicano gangs. These were the tensions the Catholic Church was trying to defuse. Instead, over the course of the 1930s, White Fence slowly moved from self-protection group to aggressive barrio gang. "By 1939 The Los Angeles Times was writing articles about the 'White Fence Gang' which murdered 2 males and left their bodies along Whittier Blvd."

Following the Depression and the exigencies of World War II, street gangs started to gain in strength again in the 1950s and 1960s, although they didn't yet function primarily as criminal organizations. This is the era of the so-called "turf gangs" memorialized in the 1961 musical *West Side Story*, which told the story of violent conflict between a white gang, the Jets, and the Puerto Rican Sharks. The musical, too, reports a story about the need for protection:

> *When you're a Jet,*
> *If the spit hits the fan,*
> *You got brothers around,*
> *You're a family man!*
>
> *You're never alone,*
> *You're never disconnected!*
> *You're home with your own:*
> *When company's expected,*
> *You're well protected!*

And, of course, the musical tells the story of ethnic competition:

The Jets are in gear,
Our cylinders are clickin'!
The Sharks'll steer clear
'Cause ev'ry Puerto Rican's a lousy chicken!

Here come the Jets
Like a bat out of hell.
Someone gets in our way,
Someone don't feel so well!

We're drawin' the line,
So keep your noses hidden!
We're hangin' a sign,
Says "Visitors forbidden"
And we ain't kiddin'!

In histories of gangs, from antiquity to the present, one finds over and over again a familiar story. As it inevitably goes, groups form in order to provide mutual protection and then, once numbers give them power, they turn to predation, particularly in moments of economic contraction. Scholars concur that this is the basic pattern, unchangeable human nature. The evidence, they say, is "overwhelming." There's also another turn of the screw. Once gangs turn predatory, they often prey mostly on their own communities. Like taxing authorities, they come to see their communities as a source of extractable revenue. This is why the stories of gangs and drugs come together. To sell drugs you need a market. A gang delivers turf and a community. It's easier to sell something illegal where you are known.

In the 1960s, gang violence intensified when eddying currents from economic privation and ethnic tension commingled once again. When postwar American prosperity inevitably turned to recession, massive war clouds of civil unrest loomed on the horizon. In 1960, the unemployment rate for adults in Harlem was about 13 percent, twice that of the rest of the city. By 1961, the number of addicts in Harlem was eight times what it was in the rest of the city. In Los Angeles, the situation was no different, and unemployment for African Americans spiraled from 12 percent to 30 percent from the late 1950s to the mid-1960s. In 1964, there were, yet again, race riots in Rochester, New York City, Philadelphia, Chicago, and Jersey City, Paterson, and Elizabeth, New Jersey, creating a litany of urban violence that would come to define the decade. In response to a national poverty rate that had reached 19 percent, Lyndon Johnson launched the War on Poverty. But still, 1965 brought the riots, rebellion, and unrest in Watts. A scuffle after the arrest of a drunk driver led to a six-day explosion of violence, arson, and conflict with police in a neighborhood stripped of resources and agency. The governor of California established a curfew of 8 P.M. across a 46.5-square-mile zone. Thirty-four people died.

In response to the violence in Watts, the Los Angeles police militarized. L.A. recruited its first SWAT team from Vietnam vets. As governor of California, Ronald Reagan advocated strict gun control to prevent Black Panthers and other African Americans from obtaining guns. Within ten years, the Los Angeles Police Department would form the first airborne police division. Its helicopters give the city's nighttime skies the distinctive thrum of a combat zone, a world Michael would be born into only five years later.

The Watts revolt of 1965 was followed, ripple-like, with more unrest in 1966 and 1967, this time in Cleveland; San Francisco; Chicago; Newark; Plainfield, New Jersey; Detroit; Harlem; Cambridge, Maryland; Rochester; Pontiac; Toledo; Flint; Grand Rapids; Houston; Englewood, New Jersey; Tucson; Milwaukee; and northerly Minneapolis-Saint Paul. The litany goes on.

The tide of violence continued to rise, cresting in 1968 when Martin Luther King, Jr., was assassinated on the balcony of a Memphis hotel room and rioting ensued in 125 cities, sending a tsunami of destruction from coast to coast.

As relative prosperity turned to privation, the street gangs depicted in *West Side Story* evolved. Martin Luther King, Jr.'s message about uniting around the table of brotherhood gave way to forceful messages about self-help. Some gangs, which had formed initially as mutual protection societies but had grown into juvenile delinquency groups, now evolved into sophisticated criminal operations seeking to capture some of the drug business. Why should the Mafia alone reap the benefits of preying on African American adversity? Why not keep the business inside the community?

In New York City, Charles Green launched the first independent black trafficking organization in the 1960s, with over one hundred distributors and couriers. His successor was a man named Leroy "Nicky" Barnes. By the time of Nicky's arrest in 1976, he owned five homes, a Mercedes, a Maserati, and several Lincolns, Cadillacs, and Thunderbirds.

Nature red in tooth and claw shows itself in the willingness of drug sellers to see addicts as fair game. Over the course of the 1950s, the ravages of addiction turned the "dope fiend" into a figure from people's nightmares, a villainous Hollywood trope, and the most despicable of human types. Consider again the words that Michael used to describe life in prison. "I'm trapped in a hell with whom society decrees to be the worst of living and better off dead. Robbers, rapists, child molesters, carjackers, murderers, and dope fiends who would spend their mother's monthly rent for a quick fix." Inspired by Dante, he offers a descending list of criminals from least bad to worst, and on his list dope fiends are the worst of the worst, the lowest of the low.

The turn by some street gangs to the drug business perverted the Malcolm X–like drive for black economic independence. But that cynicism was facilitated by a generally accepted social pattern throughout the whole country of treating addicts, and especially African American addicts, as disposable. There was little shame in preying on them, a big contrast to how heroin addicts are viewed today.

The tableaux in Philadelphia, Los Angeles, and Chicago are all similar to the New York story of Charles Green and Leroy "Nicky" Barnes. Starting in 1969, an African American group called the Black Mafia sought control of the drug market in Philadelphia; in Chicago the Black P. Stone Nation and Black Gangster Disciples also got their start, entering into the lucrative drug business in the 1970s. The Los Angeles Crips were founded in the 1960s with ties to the Black Panthers. Initially "a community based organization set up to help local residents," when one of their founders was killed in 1969 by a rival organization, they transitioned to dealing in drugs and guns. The rising class of gang-based drug dealers was dubiously glamorized in the 1972 blaxploitation film *Super Fly*.

Today, as it was then, the global drug business is an ethnically structured market, whose points of transition from one ethnic group to another come largely at either the wholesale to retail transition point, or at the retail to street-level transition point. The rule of thumb about sales in the drug business is that most users buy from people who look like themselves. The drug market is fully an equal opportunity employer, and there's a world of white distributors and independent distributors. But it's also true that the ethnically structured street gang world of the United States was a very good fit for one part of the street-level end of an intercontinental supply chain. The largest profits, of course, accrue to those working from the production to the wholesale point of the chain, but even further down the chain there was still real money to be made.

For all the profits to be had, though, not all gangs dove into the drug business, and this is an important point to remember. Other gangs focused elsewhere: on car theft or burglary or simply on partying. A study found that in Pasadena in 1995, for instance, only two out of eighteen gangs specialized in illegal narcotics. The same study found, though, that law enforcement systematically overestimated the rate of involvement of gangs in drug transactions. "'Almost all' and 'upward of 90 percent' were not uncommon estimates of the number of drug transactions that involved gang members from both gang and narcotics experts in Los Angeles." In fact, the percentage ranged between 30 and 50. But by 2016, gangs and drugs were surely even more intertwined than they had been twenty years earlier. When the global narcotics business and American street gangs joined forces in the late 1960s and 1970s, we commenced what I propose was a new American story. Call it the story of the rise of a parastate, an alternative universe of law and order, fundamentally at war with the legally recognized state. Unbeknownst to the adults around him, Michael grew up in that parastate.

So now we have our definition of gangbanging. The core element is this: protect yo turf. This is what gangs were about in the beginning, before the world was flat enough for drugs to flow so fluidly. But all three words matter: "protect" "yo" "turf." So try this on for a definition. To gangbang (v.): to protect *your* turf and use your power to prey on the vulnerable in order to make a profit and support those *whom you call your own*.

AT THIRTEEN, ROSLYN WANTED nothing more than to be a cheerleader. She—a generous, fleshy girl who wore her skirt and twirled her pom-poms with supreme self-confidence, a gorgeous smile on her face—would get her chance in ninth grade. But like Nicholas, she, too, would find that she needed to join a gang. Hers was not, though, a drug-selling gang. She joined because she was routinely bullied at school for her dark skin and wanted some people who would protect her. To join, she stepped into a stall-lined bathroom at her school and fought seven girls on the cold tiles. She fought them in order to earn their protection.

Why are these things that parents don't know about?

26.

HOW NOT TO HELP
YOUR KIDS

About when Nicholas got jumped into a gang, Karen met a new man. In the fall of 1989, she had enrolled at East Los Angeles College for a certification as a medical records accredited records technician (ART), but at the end of her first semester, in her Alcoholics Anonymous meetings, she met Henry McAdam, a jack-of-all-trades who picked up whatever work he could in construction, maintenance, and laboring. The sex was great, and they may even have been in love. As she had for Paul, she once again dropped out of school.

Michael was ten when his mother met Henry, and Michael loved him. Henry took him fishing for trout and catfish. They did many things together and spent real time, and there was a certain kind of intimacy. When she was in middle school, Roslyn used to say that she had two dreams: one, to go to Stanford and, the other, to be a stay-at-home mom and raise a family. Michael dreamed of family, too, I'm sure of it, conjuring up a stable world in his rooftop meditations. Henry stepped into the empty place Michael's riverine meditations must have carved in his soul.

I was back home from my first year at Princeton the next summer, working as an electric meter reader, racing from house to house in my little brown Southern California Edison shorts, just so I could steal a few hours reading Lincoln's speeches parked beneath a shady tree in my electrical company truck. In July, Pastor Rinehart married Karen and Henry in a simple but serious ceremony. Henry, Nicholas, and Michael looked handsome in their tuxes with big white carnations in the buttonholes. With her hair tightly pulled back, and pearls around her neck, Roslyn looked statuesque in pink satin. Karen wore antique ivory. I expect I wore a sundress. I vividly remember a spirit of triumph around the occasion, similar to Karen's graduation from nursing school. After the wedding, the new family moved to Bay Springs, Mississippi, Henry's hometown, a hamlet of about 1,500 souls, so named for mineral springs that had once been surrounded by bay trees. Here was a single mother's dream, no? First a nursing degree, then some college; followed by marriage and a move out of the city—if not to the suburbs, at least to the country.

But the dream was not to be. Even at the wedding, other emotions were also in the air. I didn't personally feel much warmth toward Henry. And there were other warning signs. Neither Nicholas nor Roslyn is smiling in the wedding photos. They look, in fact, as though they are steeling themselves against some coming torment invisible to the rest of us. Even Henry isn't really smiling in the pictures. Only Michael has a grin as broad as the dawn.

After a decade in which Karen, painstakingly and methodically, had built up her resources, income, and opportunities, she was poised to lose it all. The five of them had moved to Bay Springs, motivated at least partially by a desire to extract Nicholas from growing gang entanglements. But on the first anniversary of their move, Karen and the kids were unceremoniously back in California without the groom and with nearly all of their money, energy, and joy spent. The fifteen months with Henry were, Karen says, "The Nightmare." For all of them.

Before the wedding, Karen did not know that Henry had a criminal record and that back in his home town, he was entrapped in a dense Mississippi thicket of violence and vendetta. As it turned out, he had shot a man when he was fourteen or fifteen and had served time for it. Now that Henry was back in Bay Springs, his adversary's grandson wanted retribution. The grandson sought it by trying to rape Roslyn. Although her family pressed charges, Roslyn, then twelve, did not in the end want to go court.

There is more. Even before this new paroxysm of personal violence, Karen had had to send Nicholas to live with his grandfather, her father, for safety's sake. It turns out that Henry had already hit and gone after Nicholas in California, even before the wedding. Now, in Bay Springs, things only worsened. One night, after a long, languid day, Nicholas was sitting on the living room couch watching television. He thought he heard the sound of tussling coming from his mother's and stepfather's bedroom. Alarmed for his mother's sake, Nicholas rose and walked to where the living room met the hallway leading to the bedroom.

It couldn't have been a big house, nor a long distance. Suddenly, the door burst open and Henry flew out, coming straight for Nicholas. To this day, Nicholas doesn't know why Henry charged at him, but terror struck and he turned on his heels and ran. He thinks Henry grabbed some sort of implement, maybe a frying pan. Henry was, Karen says, trying to kill Nicholas. By that time, Henry had started to drink again and was abusing Karen, especially when he was drunk. He must have been drunk that night. Nicholas ran to the neighbors and didn't come back. So Karen had to send Nicholas away.

In exile in a strange land, Karen became focused on protecting Nicholas and then Roslyn. Ten-year old Michael wandered around on his own in the Mississippi woods. It could not have been easy for Michael, a sociable, gifted boy, to move from the urban climes of Southern California to this rural town, and to change schools after the school year had already started. But no one knows, really, what Michael's life was like during the six or seven months under the water oaks and red maples in Bay Springs. Karen's impression was that Mississippi was pretty much okay for Michael, the ten-year-old (soon to be eleven). He played a lot. There were plenty of trees to climb, nature's rooftops on which to meditate. He spent a lot of time by himself out of doors, always his favorite place to be. Karen doesn't remember with any precision what Michael was up to then. No doubt he noticed, though, when his older brother Nicholas was sent away to Georgia, like a refugee, to live with their grandfather. The boys had never before been separated.

Finally, one Mississippi evening—in April or May, not too long after the beating of Rodney King—Henry came home drunk again and in a fighting mood. This time Karen took the kids and ran. She left without her shoes. She had to sneak back to get them, her money, and their clothes. Then the three of them—Karen, Roslyn, and Michael—jumped into the car and drove.

When his mother, all of thirty-five, ran away from Henry, Michael became her boon companion. First, they escaped to his grandparents in Baxley, Georgia, yet another time-bound Southern hamlet ensconced in the deep woods. Roslyn was along for this panicked journey. Then, in June, Karen packed Roslyn off on a plane to Big Ros, to Oakland, for the summer, and took Michael, her good luck charm, to Americus, Georgia, a much bigger town with a state university 125 miles due west. She intended to reconcile with Henry, who was now staying with a brother who lived there. When Karen and Michael reconnected with Henry, though, they found that, before leaving Mississippi, Henry had matter-of-factly sold all of the children's toys. Michael was devastated. For the first time in his life he had nothing. It was one thing to lose his toys; it was quite another to find that the man who had filled the hollow place in his heart had sold them. Living wasn't easy that summertime.

By early autumn, as I was headed back to Princeton's gothic halls for my junior year, Karen pressed charges in the Americus courts for domestic abuse. Determined to leave Henry, she sued for divorce, winning alimony of $25 per week. All the while, Henry's brother stalked her, riding around in a car with a shotgun. And with this welter of violence washing over the family, Michael got into trouble for the first time. Sometime that fall, a few months shy of twelve, he stole a jar of coins, amounting to something under $10, from a white family across the street. He was starting to want things, impatiently, and he was also naïve, a little California kid, transplanted to the Deep South. Only out of naïveté could he have thought to steal anything from a white family in southern Georgia.

Rather than merely telling Karen about the theft and asking for repayment, the family pressed charges. This was the eleven-year-old's first encounter with the law. Michael—still two year's shy of his teens—went to court with his mother. By then Karen had her plane tickets to California. She duly showed those to the judge, who told her he would drop the charges, but only if she would get on the plane and never come back.

Once more, with the school year already having started, the family was in flight. George H. W. Bush happened to be president and was celebrating the triumph of Ronald Reagan's family values. But the touters of marriage as the solution to the single mother's woes neglect a fundamental point: the quality of the man makes all the difference. Henry ripped through their lives like a Mississippi twister.

Between the 1990 wedding and the summer of 1993, when Karen was finally resettled in Los Angeles with a measure of stability in a job that she would hold for more than a decade, Karen would go through four jobs and the kids through six mid-year school transitions.

These were the years that Michael grew from eleven to fourteen. This is clearly when things went wrong.

27.

THE LIMIT ON HELPING
YOUR KIDS

Pre-adolescence is when the trouble started, when Michael was eleven and his mother's brief marriage to Henry came apart before it even really began. Now began Karen's journey through multiple jobs and the kids' journeys through multiple schools. After Bay Springs, Baxley and Americus, now, once again, a month into the school year, in October 1991, just before his twelfth birthday, Michael moved. This time he and his family moved from Georgia to Claremont, the California college town modeled on Oxford and Cambridge, where I grew up and where my political scientist father, a Reagan appointee on the U.S. Civil Rights Commission with one more year to serve, lived and taught.

My brother and I were by then away at college, but my parents, Uncle William and Aunt Susan, a librarian at one of the local colleges, were still there and for my cousins their house was a second home, screened with laurel bushes, framed by pink-blossomed crepe myrtles, and shaded by a spreading loquat tree in front. In the back, I recall, was a glorious female ginko that burst into a bright gold blaze every year around Thanksgiving. Stinko ginko, I always called the fertile tree, for its raunchy-smelling fruits. Just past it was my mother's rose garden, a hammock along one side.

My parents helped Karen find an apartment a few blocks away, the kind Southern California is full of, a modest two-story frame building, with walk-up apartments. Michael took piano lessons with a stern, diminutive woman who had been my own teacher and who taught us how to listen. She also taught hand position and demanded that we sit up straight, "like the Queen of England." Michael earned money gardening for her, but resented the hectoring lessons about life that this martinet of a lady delivered standing over him as he weeded. This comfortable college town, where I went to public school, captained the track and volleyball teams, and learned how to hide my big vocabulary, is also where Roslyn fought her way into a gang to get protection from bullying.

With a November birthday, Michael was, like me, always young for his class. When he arrived in Claremont, he was already in seventh grade. He made a friend, Adam, but the two of them got in trouble together in school. They were caught stealing chocolate chip cookies from the school cafeteria. They made noise in class. They sometimes had to be separated. The school wanted to put Michael on Ritalin, but Karen was worried about drugs and declined.

Karen came home one day and found Michael gone. "Mama, I messed up at school again, and I know I can't do what you want, so I'm leaving," he'd penned in a note. He had skipped school, packed his hand-me-down suitcase, and gone to a friend's house for dinner, before heading to his family's church, which was my family's church, too, to spend the night. He was found there before the night was very far advanced, and the next day he was back in school, after just a single day's absence. His whole class gave him a card saying, "Welcome Home." This, his mother takes it, was evidence of how beloved he was.

Michael was also caught shoplifting at a nearby mall during this time. Unlike that Georgia family, the store owner delivered Michael to my father, not the police. Michael's pattern of petty theft increasingly worried my father. The weeding job was intended to be part of a solution to Michael's need for money. The pattern also worried Karen. She signed him up for a program called "Simba," run by affiliates of the Nation of Islam based in Pomona, a town just to the south, further from the hills, and on the other side of the 10 Freeway. She hoped that they could help instill discipline. With Simba, Michael stood on the street corner, selling bean pies. As with the peanut sales in Highland Park, he was good at selling things and seemed to enjoy it.

He also played on the school football team and was good at that, too. For Michael, that activity brought joy alongside the discipline.

But once again fire struck the tragedy-prone family in early 1993. This time their apartment complex went up in flames, caused by a smoker's accident or something electrical. My parents had by now moved to Michigan, so the anchor had been pulled out, and with their unit condemned for smoke damage, they found themselves homeless. For the first week or so after

MICHAEL ON A
JUNIOR HIGH
FOOTBALL TEAM

the fire, they scattered, each spending the night on a different friend's couch. Then Karen got a Red Cross voucher and
began to look for a new place to live.

A few months before the fire, she had started a new job,
for an organization called Homeless Healthcare in Los Angeles. Wanting to keep the kids in school, she had been making
the thirty-five-mile commute from Claremont to Los Angeles each day. But now, with the need to find a new place to
live and my parents resettled in the Midwest, Karen decided
to move back to Los Angeles, a charred city after the Rodney
King riots, to be closer to her work. By May, she'd gotten all
of them but Nicholas—who continued to stay with a family

friend—into a house in Inglewood, a neighborhood still try-ing to lift its head up from the ravages of the previous year's waves of angry violence.

We know something about Michael's school experience during eighth grade because the State of California decided to survey its youth just then. The officials discovered something that any of the kids themselves could have told them: the kids were drowning in violence. According to the report, in the 1993–94 school year, 39.8 percent of ninth graders reported being in a physical fight, while 57.3 percent reported seeing someone at school with a weapon. The report also revealed that 16 percent of seventh-graders, 18 percent of ninth-graders, and 16 percent of eleventh-graders reported having belonged to a gang at some time in their life. This is an extremely high rate of vulnerability for an adolescent population. Even in the verdant college town of Claremont, gangs, as Roslyn learned, were a factor. We have to infer that all these statistics would have been still higher in the most urbanized settings, such as Michael's new school in Inglewood. Of course, many students, like my brother and me, were able to deal with vulnerability without joining a gang. But for some significant number of young people, the gang was the solution to this experience of vulnerability. Gangs filled in for family.

After they moved to Inglewood, with just a few months of the year left, neither Michael nor his sister, having been uprooted so many times, could be bothered to go to school. The truancy officer, whom their own mother dispatched after them, never seemed able to catch up with them. Michael, now just shy of fourteen, seems to have flirted with a local gang, the Queen Street Bloods, a black street gang located on the west side of Inglewood that warred with the Raymond Avenue Crips.

Bloods vs. Crips. Red vs. Blue. That was the most important political division for black kids growing up in South Central. According to another cousin, kids in Bloods neighborhoods grew up with a lesson seared into their minds, "Blue is bad. Blue is bad. Blue is bad. Red is good. Red is good. Red is good." Kids in Crips neighborhoods clung to the opposite mantra.

As he played hooky and roamed the streets, Michael was testing out a new world. But he also spent time that summer of 1993 returning to his old one. He often rode the big white RTD bus thirty-five miles back out to Claremont to hang out with Adam, with whom he stole the neighbor's radio on one of those visits. That's when he earned his two-year probation.

The narrative so far is recognizable. A kid from a troubled home, trapped in poverty, without a stable world of adults coordinating care for him, starts pilfering, mostly out of an impatience to have things. Up to this point, Michael's tale includes not a single story of violence perpetrated by him other than the usual squabbles and wrestling matches with siblings. From here, any number of possible endings are still imaginable. But however broad the horizon of the imagination may be, events themselves unfold along a single track. Life may be a choose-your-own-adventure game, but we can live but one life. As we go, we shed all the other lives that might have been. From fourteen, Michael's path ran from a broad horizon up and through difficult and merciless terrain.

In his fifteenth year, fewer than four years after he had

stolen a jar of coins in Georgia, Michael's life accelerated in its seriousness, instantly, into prison and beyond, like one of those pneumatic tubes whisking off your deposit at a drive-thru bank.

For the final year before Michael's arrest, just to understand how that acceleration could happen, we need a new kind of narrative. This calls for the story of the parastate.

28.

CITY OF ANGELS

Consider the visible surface of Los Angeles. Freeway underpasses, bridges, alleyways, delivery trucks, service entrances, corner convenience stores, mailboxes, water towers, exhaust vents, and streets—except for those in the poshest parts of town, all are covered with graffiti. This was even truer in the 1990s, before the city achieved true expertise in pushing graffiti to the backs of signs and to the margins of freeways, instead of their main walls.

Can you read the graffiti? I couldn't then and have only now barely begun to learn how to decipher it. But it's a language and represents a world. It records deaths and transactions, favors done and owed, benefactions and trespasses. Laws and punishments. If you can't read that graffiti, you have no idea what's happening around you. How can anyone guide the young who can't read the navigational charts?

When Karen moved her family back to Los Angeles, they

hadn't lived there in seven years, not since 1986. These were the very years in which the twisting double helix of drugs and gangs converged with an evolution in the criminal justice system. Now, under the mantle of the War on Drugs, came the state's strongest push for deterrence. With that push, specific human beings, each victim, every wrongdoer, disappeared from the story of crime.

As I mentioned, a 1995 study found that law enforcement systematically overestimated the rate of involvement of gangs in drug transactions. As policy-makers sought to crack down on drugs, it seemed easy to do that just by cracking down on gangs. Because the drug business was erroneously attributed almost entirely to gangs, the War on Drugs morphed into a War on Gangs. The consequences of this transformation have come to define the criminal justice system.

A full decade earlier, in 1984, as Nancy Reagan was teaching people to "Just Say No," the Drug Enforcement Administration initiated Operation Pipeline to interdict drug trafficking on the nation's highways through the use of traffic stops. This operation, introduced in the get-tough era of President Reagan, provided national training for police in what we have come to know as racial profiling. Between 1984 and 1988, the State of California also passed eighty separate antigang measures, many of which added "enhancements" to sentences for any case that involved a gang element, a nice euphemism for giving someone extra years in prison. It must be said that getting tough on crime was a fully bipartisan pursuit. Democrats, as well as Republicans, drove through laws like these across all the states and at the federal level. A favorite tool was to pass a law mandating the minimum sentence for a specific crime, and thereby stripping judges of the discretion to peg a penalty to the circumstances of the wrongdoer.

From 1790 to 1950 the number of mandatory minimums in the federal penal code rose from 7 to 38. From 1980 to 2000, their number rose from 77 to 284. These mandatory minimums have been a key driver in increases in penal severity.

In these years, twenty-five years after the Jets and the Sharks stormed Broadway, the Los Angeles County Sheriff's Department created its first gang database. In 1988, after a high-profile drive-by shooting of a bystander near UCLA, the Los Angeles police used that database to round up no fewer than 1,400 African American youth in the L.A. Coliseum and to jail over 18,000 people in six months. One year later, the Los Angeles police chief, Daryl Gates, testified to the Senate Judiciary Committee that "the casual drug user should be taken out and shot." The African American prison population in California alone grew from 12,470 to 42,296 between 1982 and 1995; the Latino prison population soared from 9,006 to 46,080. This was the city ready to explode when the four police officers who had been captured on video beating Rodney King were acquitted. This was the City of Angels.

Karen and her brood came home to a war between two sovereigns: the parastate of a drug world increasingly linked to gangs on one side, and the California and federal governments on the other. When Michael stole that $10 in Georgia, and the judge dropped the charges, you might say Michael met the "forgiving world." When he shoplifted and stole the radio in Claremont in 1993, and didn't get any actual charges, you might again say that he met a "forgiving world." But by 1993, back in Los Angeles, Michael met a politically transformed world that was now unforgiving. By 1995, when he was arrested for the first time for the attempted carjacking and the previous day's robberies, the angels had already turned their backs.

Yet it is not enough merely to see the parastate or to record the emergence of the unforgiving world. We must notice something else. I ask you this: how could Karen have known the landscape into which she was now moving her family? She was coming, once again, for a job. As had been the case in 1979, the City of Angels, with its rapidly increasing population and growing service industries, drew her siren-like with its opportunity. That opportunity was clear to her. The parastate was not.

The historian's backward gaze can capture the life-altering convergence of the drug business, gangs, and a newly unforgiving criminal justice system, but while you're living through it, only the smallest fragments—like news reports about crime— are visible. Fragments like police willing to round up 1,400 black men at one time.

Like the Los Angeles riots or, as some call them, rebellions.

Like miles of graffiti.

But what exactly do these fragments amount to? How can we know when we're living through it? What is the name of the problem? As Karen navigated these turbulent waters, always seeking to pilot her vulnerable boatload of kids toward refuge, she could see only a bit of the whale's tail here, a flash of fin there, and now and then the arching crest of the back breaking from the waves. But the whole beast? Never.

What was the beast, exactly, which now and then knocked her small craft? The graffiti is the clue. It records, yes, a world of violence and vendettas, with pregnant histories and decipherable rules. With benefactions and trespasses, crimes and punishments. A world in its own valence with its own laws.

The state sought to break the global drug supply chain by rounding up the lowest-level peddlers and assigning them disproportionate penalties in order to deter them. But too much money was at stake for the producers and wholesalers merely to concede defeat and cede control of their retail and street distributors. By the estimates of federal prosecutors, the famous "Freeway Rick," an L.A. high school tennis star and community college upholstery student, made about $850 million between 1982 and 1989 selling cocaine to both Bloods and Crips gangs. The producers and wholesalers would fight rather than cave in to the government's efforts to strip them of their distributors. They needed retailers and street sellers who could guarantee recruits into the business and also enforce discipline. To fight back against the War on Drugs, the drug gangs who took the business seriously established their own system of deterrence.

In short, if you don't do what you're supposed to do, you're shot immediately. In the knee first. You try to buck again? Then maybe you're killed. Or maybe someone you love is killed. Immediately. The drug business depends on well-documented witness suppression programs. It operates a far more powerful system of deterrence than any a lawful state could ever devise. This is, finally, what makes it the parastate.

And then there's another wrinkle. The War on Drugs has overloaded the justice system with nonviolent drug offenses.

In U.S. district courts in 2013, 32 percent of defendant filings were for drug-related cases, making this the biggest category of filings. State judicial systems, too, have been significantly strained for financial resources and personnel by drug-related casework, and this has been true since the early 1990s. An overloaded judicial system then appears to put prosecutors in a position where, with regard to violent crimes, they wish to pursue only open-and-shut cases that will generate plea deals. According to Vernon Geberth, a retired police officer interviewed on public radio, police nowadays have a higher bar to get over in trying to clear homicides, for instance, because prosecutors want only those easier cases.

This higher bar has further effects. When it's harder for police to hand over cases to prosecutors, we see declines in homicide clearance rates, the percentage of homicide cases that result in closed cases. What's more, even those clearance rates mask failures because cases are often closed without an arrest or prosecution. In the 1960s, for instance, the average clearance rate for homicide was above 90 percent. In contrast, in Detroit in the years approaching the city's bankruptcy, the homicide clearance rate verged on single digits. In Chicago in 2009, police cleared only 30 percent of homicide cases, many of them without charges. And in one Los Angeles Police Department bureau, clearance rates at about 60 percent hide the low rate of cases ending in arrest and prosecution. Clearance rates are lowest when victims are black and brown.

The consequences of falling clearance rates, especially against a backdrop of a narcotics business driving increases in violence, are profound. Pay close attention to Michael's trajectory from 1991 through 1995. He stole $10 in coins from neighbors across the street; then he shoplifted and stole a radio from a next-door neighbor; then he acquired a gun and held up at gunpoint at least three and possibly five people in a one-week stretch. The dates are linear but the increase in the magnitude of his actions is exponential. This acceleration caught the adults in Michael's life off guard. They were working to push back at the trouble, but they thought the pace of the battle was arithmetic, a matter of mere addition. They expected that the next event might be, at worst, one unit more serious than the previous. Instead, there was a phase shift. How do we explain this acceleration in Michael's life?

To write this biography of the parastate, we will have to turn, forgive me, to economics. Two economists, Brendan O'Flaherty and Rajiv Sethi, have pinpointed an incredibly subtle connection between the War on Drugs and violence. They argue that above-average homicide rates—that is, above-average rates of armed violence and especially gun violence—will result from low rates of successful investigation and prosecution of homicide cases. If you live in an environment where you know that someone can shoot you with impunity, you are much more likely to be ready to shoot to kill at the first sign of danger. When murder goes unpunished, it begets more murder, partly for purposes of retaliation, partly because people are emboldened by lawlessness, but also as a matter of preemption. Unpunished murder makes everyone (including police) trigger-happy. Places where murder goes unpunished operate according to the dictum that the best defense is a strong offense. In other words, in places with low homicide clearance rates, there is a phase shift in the level of violence in the environment, and not simply a linear progression. Guns spread. The world tips from one social equilibrium to another. This phase shift, the rapid descent through a tipping point, is what we experience as acceleration. This is why the experience feels like that pneumatic tube whisking us instantly up a chute. This phase shift explains the acceleration in Michael's life.

I've asked people who grew up in South Central how Michael might have gotten his gun. No one can give me a specific answer. This is not because they don't know but because, as they incessantly say, "But guns are so easy to get. He could get a gun from just about anybody." It's my question—of how could Michael have gotten a gun—that doesn't make any sense. It's a stupid question. Guns were, simply stated, a matter of course in Los Angeles in the early 1990s.

My cousin Roslyn tells a surreal story. She was at a party once, somewhere in L.A., when someone came in and dumped a black garbage bag full of hard objects out onto the middle of the floor. Guns spilled out. Another girl grabbed one and held it to Roslyn's head.

"Are you Blood? Are you Blood?" she demanded.

Roslyn, petrified, said nothing. Then, a man she'd never seen, and has never seen again, a ghost dressed all in white, suddenly appeared. "She's cool," the apparition said and disappeared. The girl lowered the gun and Roslyn left.

In urban centers of the global drug trade, such as the City of Angels, a parastate now operates a system of deterrence even more powerful than a legitimate state can operate. In addition, the misguided policies of the War on Drugs have themselves contributed to an acceleration of violence. Tragically, this simply entrenches the power of the parastate, which over and over again gains its first recruits because they need protection.

I am trying to make visible something that remains even to this day invisible.

It is not invisible because I am bad at seeing.

It is not invisible because I am bad at hunting.

It is not invisible because I am bad at researching.

I don't fail to see its whole shape because I am oblivious or keeping my head in the sand. The beast below the turbulent waters of Los Angeles is invisible because it is illegal. We have made the beast invisible by desiring drugs and making our own desire illegal. We have made the beast invisible by lying to ourselves in this country about who we are.

We can even measure the size of this invisible world. For each of the last ten years, Americans have annually spent an estimated $100 billion on illegal narcotics. We are, remember, the leading consumer in the world. This annual expense is one-sixth of our national budget for defense. Or put it this way: it is roughly double the annual budget of the CIA. Imagine all the covert activity the CIA conducts all over the globe. Double it. And then imagine it all happening here, at home, in the U.S. of A. This is the size of the invisible world, an invisible world far more powerful than the CIA. And we expect a small intervention here, a small charitable act there, to rescue people? The angels have turned their backs. They have turned their backs on people trapped between the warring states. And thus many millions are gone.

As we now know, when Karen moved Michael back to Los Angeles, where she had steady employment, the police had 47 percent of African American men in Los Angeles between the ages of twenty-one and twenty-four in their gang database. Reread that. In 1992, the Los Angeles Police Department had 47 percent of African American men between the ages of twenty-one and twenty-four in their gang database. It doesn't really matter if that many young men were actually gangbanging or if it was merely that the police believed them to be doing so. Nor does it matter if all of these young men were selling drugs or were only believed by the police to be doing so. In the context of residential segregation, the logic of social networks is such that once half of a particular group of young men in a city either are or are thought by the police to be involved in gangs, either are or are thought by the police to be involved in selling drugs, all of the young men in that group in the city will be affected by the world of gangs and the punishments applied to it. The question was not whether to live in this world, but only whether it could be survived. Survival would have required Michael to stay indoors, alone every day, or to have ventured out every day never any further than to his rooftop.

Some do survive, and you will find, I think, that they have often stayed indoors.

When Karen did move her family back to Los Angeles, blindly, she had to help her kids navigate a world she could not see. She could not see it because it was and is illegal. Prohibition incapacitates parents. It deepens the dark secrecy of adolescence. In the absence of a clear line of sight, meaningful choice-making is impossible, for parents and also for the young. If a person has been blindfolded, do we fault them for falling into the pit?

29.

THE END

I headed off to England for graduate school after graduating from Princeton in June 1993. Michael and Roslyn were dodging the truancy officer that same month. By the fall, Nicholas and Roslyn had both dropped out of school and left home. Nicholas was living with a friend of his mother's and hanging out with his girlfriend who, after graduating from Claremont High, had moved, too, and not very far away from where he was in downtown L.A. Roslyn headed to a Jobs Corp program in San Diego. Karen's kids were mostly grown. Only Michael, her baby, was left, the youngest child of a family's youngest daughter.

Karen of course apprehended that the frequent disruptions in Michael's life were dangerous. As she had done for him over and over, she sought continuity and she sought men. Believing he would be better off if he kept up his Nation of Islam connections with the men in Simba, she decided to send him back to Claremont for his freshman year of high school. Through the men from Simba, Karen found him a placement in Pomona in a homestay with a woman they trusted.

But the woman, as it turned out, had a son and the son was a gangbanger. When the woman agreed to take Michael in, the son wasn't living at home. But then he returned. Michael liked hanging out with him, so Karen wanted Michael out of that environment. To remove him from danger, she brought him home again to her in the middle of the school year, just after the Northridge earthquake.

Karen didn't, however, bring Michael back to the Inglewood neighborhood, where he had been flirting with the Queen Street Bloods. With her eldest child now living with his girlfriend, her girl off to Jobs Corp, and her baby gone to Pomona, Karen had thought she had an empty nest. She had given up her expensive three-bedroom $1,000-a-month house in Inglewood in favor of a small one-bedroom apartment on Imperial Highway, blocks away from where she'd first moved the big kids and baby Michael when they set out on their journey as a family. Now, when Michael returned to her, she enrolled her precocious baby in an advanced college program at nearby Southwest Community College, a program for high school students that gets them through their high school curriculum and into the first phase of college all in four years. This seemed like a reasonable choice, but deep down Karen was still a country girl. She didn't know that Southwest Community College was Crips territory, and that these gangs were bigger, stronger, and more violent than those in the Inglewood neighborhood.

Leaving Pomona, Michael moved with Karen to the apartment on Imperial Highway. Almost up under the freeway overpass, the apartment, nondescript in a concrete landscape, stewed in car exhaust. There were no trees here; no rooftops worthy of meditation. But Southwest seemed to give Michael what he needed: books and the outdoors. The soon-to-be fifteen-year-old flourished in his classes and joined the cross-country team, even running the 1995 L.A. Marathon with the team, fueled by his mom's pasta dinner.

And he had a new chance to travel. Karen had earned her state license as a minister and was beginning to fly regularly to women's leadership conferences. Michael went with her to D.C., Oakland, and San Diego.

Then came Michael's junior year. During the summer before it began, he had looked for jobs. He tried grocery stores, seeking work as a stock boy or bag boy. His older cousin Marc had worked in a grocery store as a bag boy throughout his high school years. But Michael had no luck. At fifteen, he needed a work permit to work and he didn't have one. Nor did he find an employer willing to work around that. His mother's social network didn't have anyone in it who could offer him a job either. In July, he went to Michigan for a couple of weeks to visit his Uncle William, Aunt Susan, and cousin Marc, himself now also a Princeton graduate. Michael admired his cousin's forest green Volkswagen Passat.

Michael spent that August back home again, and now, once again, began to cause his mother worry. On those warm summer days, sometimes reaching 90 degrees, he maximized his time out of doors. He would leave the apartment and roam. Sometimes, four blocks away from their apartment, he would stand out in front of the house of a kid he'd come to know. His mother spotted him, lean and muscled from his long-distance running, standing shirtless in khaki trousers. This was gang-banging gear.

"There were two guys standing there and their parents. They had on t-shirts, and one of them had a hairnet. It just represented the wrong environment," she recalls. "You live up under the freeway bypass, not here," she chastised him. Although he was standing only four blocks away from her apartment, it felt like a different neighborhood. When she asked him what he was doing, Michael answered, "Nothing, Mom. I'm just hot."

Michael's sister Roslyn, now seventeen, and discovering boys, was also home that August. They spent time together. Michael was out and about all over the neighborhood, she realized. He'd acquired a friend, Devonn, who was a Crip. They had actually met at church. This friend was a member of the Rollin 60s Crips, just as, according to some people, the pastor Andrew Rinehart had once been. With this knowledge, the blue décor of Rinehart's church takes on a different meaning. About Pastor Rinehart, another cousin says: "When he practiced his ministry, he practiced it in these disenfranchised neighborhoods with these young people who needed help. These young kids who do participate in these activities still needed some place to go."

Michael wasn't sensitive to the blue-red color code. He understood it, but he didn't feel it in his flesh. This is what his sister means when she says he was all over the neighborhood. He was crossing color lines. He hung out with Devonn, a Crip, but Roslyn also spotted him hanging out down the street from their mom's apartment on Imperial in khakis and a red shirt, presumably a vestige of his association with the Queen Street Bloods. His sister marveled that he was able to move so fluidly through different territories, each of which should have been off-limits to someone who had been hanging in one of the other territories. One day he did come home with a black eye. He'd taken a beating for refusing to join a gang, he told her.

Another cousin, Pili, who was just two months older than Michael and who lived only a few blocks away, tells yet another story of what Michael was up to. He recalls riding the bus with his cousin back to the old Inglewood neighborhood and watching Michael get jumped back into the Queen Street Bloods. He says there were two different ways of relating to gangs. If you grew up in a neighborhood, you just were part of that gang and you didn't have to do anything to prove your affiliation, so you could get away without gangbanging. But if you were a newcomer, someone who had moved around a lot, then, wherever you landed, you would have to prove yourself, clarify your loyalties, and declare your allegiances with actions. Michael was in this situation, Pili recalls.

Sometime that summer before their junior year, Michael and Pili both ended up spending the night at another uncle's house. Probably they'd gone there to swim. The last week of August and first week of September brought an unbroken string of hot days. Karen happened to be out of town. Before the boys went to sleep, Michael said to Pili, "If I go out in the night, tell someone." Michael didn't go out, but Pili wishes he had told someone what Michael had said.

This is how Pili began to get a sense of the trouble brewing around Michael. Something else caught his attention, too. Michael had begun calling him "Cuz." This is what members of the Crips call one another. Pili had grown up in and still lived in a Blood neighborhood. He never gangbanged, but even so the word "Cuz" discomfited him. "I can't say the word," he admits. Michael didn't feel the force of these allegiances in his flesh, Pili realized, or Michael never would have called him this. But from Michael's use of this word, Pili also realized that Michael did have some real involvement with the Crips as well as with the Bloods.

Up until the end of his life, Michael often called me "Cuz." I never knew it had this other meaning, and the gang salutation wasn't how he was using it for me. But it was a clue I might have seen and didn't.

Nicholas tells the story of his younger brother's summer and start of junior year differently yet again. By now Nicholas—nineteen years old—lived in San Pedro with his girlfriend, Sharon, and their infant daughter. He'd finished his Army Reserve training the previous spring, and was now looking for a job as a security guard while also keeping up his monthly Reserve training sessions. Michael was developing something of a relationship with Sharon's older sister, Linda, and sometimes he joined all of them in San Pedro. To Nicholas's eye, Michael was thriving. He was doing well in the new school program at Southwest College. He was running track. Michael never wore colors or other gang clothing. He seemed to have avoided full-fledged gang membership. But he had "bread"; he had the clothes and shoes that he wanted. Nicholas didn't think anything of it. He remembers one incident, though, that brought fear. He, too, had an experience standing on the street with Michael just outside his mother's apartment on Imperial.

Fool in a brown Cadillac rolled up. Guys from Denver
Lane rolled up, banging on us. Guy's holding like he's
ready to draw. Michael had some nice clothes. We knew
if we said the wrong thing or did the wrong thing, I
knew it would be a bust. "Ugly Cuz. Are you all Cuz?"
He was saying this and that. He just saw two dudes that
he didn't know.

Nicholas had known about Michael's flirtation with the Queen
Street Bloods, but he had thought it was over. He knew he
didn't have any involvement with the Denver Lane Bloods.
And it never occurred to him that his brother might be developing an association with the Crips.

Karen's story, too, possessed its own contours. She never
suspected Michael of participating in gangs. He didn't wear
colors that she ever saw. He didn't have any of the outward
telltale signs. He was doing well in school. He seemed to be off
to a good start in his junior year. She worried when she saw
him hanging out in the wrong place, but she was concerned
about what *might* happen, not about what *was* happening. She
had enough confidence in Michael that she traveled to Florida
at summer's end seeking answers to lingering questions about
how her mother's long-ago death from gallbladder surgery.
She left $500 in her bedroom, the rent money, and asked Ros-
lyn and Michael to give it to the landlady.

But when she returned, the money was gone, and the
landlady hadn't been paid. The screen door was damaged and
her bedroom had been turned topsy-turvy. Karen suspected
Michael of faking a break-in and taking the money.

A week or so later, Michael brought Karen $500. "To help

you with the rent," he said. When she asked him where he got it, he wouldn't say. She refused it, telling him, "It's blood money."

Then Michael started spending time out after his curfew. His mother thought about calling his probation officer, but a friend from her church counseled her against it. He had begun the semester earning straight A's on quizzes in his math class, but then the grade suddenly dropped down to an F. Karen had conferences with Michael and his teachers. They told him that he was smarter than this, but he countered, "I don't want to be smarter than this."

Her last day with her boy was Friday, September 15. Michael didn't have school. He went to work with his mother, and after he spent some time hanging out in her office, she took him over to the Los Angeles Public Library, which was not far from where she worked. That Friday was payday, and the plan was for Michael to meet up with her at the close of business for a shopping trip. He wanted new pants. They were supposed to meet right in the library where she had left him. Michael was gone, though, when his mother went back for him. "I know where I left him. I was there and he wasn't there." She is adamant.

In the days before cell phones, Michael and his mother had no easy way to reconnect. After an exhausting day at work, she went home, leaving a message for Michael just in case.

Michael eventually did make it back to her office. Her coworkers relayed to Michael the message that he should head on home by bus, which he didn't do. We do know he came to the neighborhood, but he didn't go home. He did catch a glimpse of his mother driving up the street, perhaps having gone out on another errand, but he ducked into a laundromat to hide. She caught a glimpse of him, too, through the window, and went around the block to check, but when he saw her car come round again, he dodged behind the machines.

After the laundromat, he went to Devonn's house, his friend who was a member of the Rollin 60s Crips. That Friday night, Devonn's mother mentioned to Karen at church that Michael had been at her house that day.

Karen asked that she send him home, but Michael did not come home.

Nor did he come on Saturday. Karen next knew about Michael only when Devonn's sister knocked on the door on Sunday morning and told Karen that her baby had been shot.

In the ambulance, Michael told his own story quite differently. He said that he had not been home for a week. He said he had found the gun two and a half weeks earlier. This would have been just when the rent money disappeared. He said first that he found the gun behind a McDonald's near his mother's house, and then changed his story to say that he found it in a garbage bag full of clothes on a walkway running alongside one of the Rosecrans apartments. Perhaps he was trying to protect his mother by putting more distance between her and his activities.

Michael, it seems, stole his mother's rent money to buy a gun. This must have had something to do with his deepening gang affiliation. He had had an acknowledged association with the Queen Street Bloods. Yet he also called the people around him, including his cousins, "Cuz." And on that September morning, he was out and about seeking revenue and action with a Crip. The police, though, never identified the crime as gang-related; next to the question "Gang member?" on their report, they checked no.

Michael was not in their gang database, nor did he ever, when he finally did get tattoos, ink in a gang symbol. He wasn't actually prepared that mid-September morning to be violent. He had acquired a gun, but he did not use it. He held back, it seems, and got shot. Stealing was in him. That we can see. But shooting was not, not then. The gun sounds most of all like somebody else's idea of what Michael needed to do to prove himself.

ALREADY WELL ON ITS way to swallowing the millions now gone, the parastate, the invisible world of the gangs, had also ensnared Michael. We can be sure of this because he never revealed the name of his accomplice.

I was able to ferret out his accomplice's first name only after Michael's death, interviewing members of our extended family. Even to this day, I have not been able to track down his last name. In his hospital conversation with the police, Michael protected himself not one whit. Although he told the police everything else, about his friend he was silent. Since he displayed a singular lack of an instinct for self-protection, he must have held this information back for reasons other than concern for his own well-being. He must have believed that if he gave the police this information, not he himself but his family would suffer retribution. For Devonn, the protective power of the gang served its purpose, at least in the short term. This is what protection in the mid-1990s in Los Angeles had come to mean.

After Michael's arrest, Karen was devastated. We all were. Karen wanted to get him out on bail, but he told her that, no, he didn't want that. He thought if he were back on the streets, he would just end up in more trouble. In choosing jail instead of the streets, in rejecting his gang entanglements, Michael at fifteen, in this moment of his first arrest, chose the seeming protection of the criminal justice system over any offer of protection from a gang.

The justice system had no interest in recognizing and responding to that choice. It was the bravest decision he ever made, yet it did not serve him well. There were few rewards for virtue when it briefly flashed in his unforgiving world.

NOW, AT LAST, WE'VE found our answer. When Michael was fifteen, both fire and ice hastened his destruction. The desire for bread was fire. Two warring systems of hate—the parastate and a metastasizing penal state—made ice. The latter, all on its own, would have sufficed.

> Temptations, hidden snares often take us unawares.
> And our hearts are made to bleed for a thoughtless word
>   or deed.
> And we wonder why the test when we try to do our best.
> But we'll understand it by and by.

Only on his rooftop, meditating, slipping the chains of desire and evading the menacing forces of hate, could Michael, possibly, have survived.

30.

MY HEART'S LOCKET

In my heart's locket, five gangly brown-skinned kids, cousins, will be forever at play in a pair of crepe myrtle trees bathed in beneficent June sunshine. I loved to climb trees as much as Michael. An arm here, a leg there, juts out from the trees' floral sundress, a delicate skein of pink and purple blooms. When we found unbloomed buds on the dichondra lawn, we would gently press at their nub until the skin slit and a fragile, crinkled blossom emerged whole. Meanwhile, inside the house, through the living room picture window, the adults, beloved, are forever passing their time in glancing, distracted talk.

Coda

WHAT NEXT?

Dearly beloved, if you ask yourself why the least among us are not thriving, you can turn the question this way and that, you can push it and you can pull it, but if you are honest, you will have to recognize that there is only one answer. The least among us are not thriving because those at the top of the illegal drug economy have established a parastate and entrapped impoverished communities within it through the systematic application of violence.

From prison and in love with Bree, on Juneteenth, a holiday that marks the date in 1865 when news finally reached Texas that all slaves were free, Michael rapped:

> *Everyone wants to be a "g" but no one wants to be a man*
> *How do I stand when these grown men wanna play*
> *   games*
> *I got to pray to fight from goin' insane*

Dearly beloved, if you ask yourself why the least among us are not thriving, you can turn the question this way and that, you can push it and you can pull it, but if you are fair, you will have to recognize that there is only one answer. The least among us are not thriving because national governments have sought to fight the War on Drugs by concentrating their world historic levels of firepower, punishment, and control on impoverished communities trapped by the systematic application of violence within the parastate.

> *Alive and well with anotha chance to get it right*
> *Despite what the media sells, we got to fight*
> *(Chorus: Respect it. Don't take it for granted.*
> *Keep it real and know that you can handle it.(4x))*
> *It represents my liberty and my ability*
> *To stand amongst those who for a second dare to hate me*
> *For the color of my skin, you can't win*
> *That's what they whisper, but I was raised completely*
>   *different.*
> *I'm on this mission, keepin' this vision*
> *Establish by those before, who now, no longer living*
> *But the spirit of freedom is far from dead*
> *Incarcerated but they can't trap what's inside of my head*

Dearly beloved, if you ask yourself why the least among us are not thriving, you can turn the question this way and that, but if you are self-aware, you will have to recognize that there is only one answer. The least among us are not thriving because so very many of us desire illegal drugs and turn a blind eye to the costs involved in supplying our desire. We are like nineteenth-century Englishmen and -women who sweetened their tea with sugar made by slaves.

> *So I smash debilitating curses*
> *Debilitating my foes wit prayer and that's for certain*
> *I'm searchin' even though I'm lock down*
> *Remaining focus and gettin' ready for when I touch down*

Dearly beloved, remember that there are three categories of direct victim of the international drug economy: ONE, addicts; TWO, victims of violence; THREE, those entrapped in the parastate. In terms of sheer numbers, the third category may be the largest. There are many millions gone.

> *They can't hold us, we under a creed*
> *I serve Christ, and like Him for my people I'll bleed*
> *Imagine if Malcolm or Martin would have gave up*
> *But in adversity they stayed down and was trued up*
> *Dearly beloved, we're today*
> *Gathered in the memory of those who were brutally*
> *   slayed*
> *I pray that we can find peace*
> *Cause even in Penitentiaries we still can remain free*
> *But there must be recognition that Prison isn't living.*

Consider the numbers of Americans now imprisoned. One out of every one hundred adult Americans is in prison. This makes more than 2 million people currently incarcerated. The world has never seen a penal system like this before.

Been down since 15, now I'm 23
   Wit 3 to go I'm ready to accept responsibility

Consider America's preeminence in imprisoning people. Twenty-five percent of the world's prisoners are in American prisons even though only about 5 percent of the world's population lives between our shining shores. The world has never seen anything like this.

This my first and last time, prison will never be
      a pastime
   A free man so you can never take mine

Consider, once more, how the War on Drugs bloats and disables the judicial system. It's so important as to be worth repeating. Fourteen percent of Americans now imprisoned have been sentenced for nonviolent drug offenses. In recent years, as many as 32 percent of defendant filings in federal courts, in a given year, are for drug-related cases. This is the biggest category of filings. And then there are all the violent offenses that flow from the intertwining double helix of drugs and gangs. Imagine how well our courts might work if this burden were removed.

The same goes for you, cause only you can stop you
   You can make or break you, so to thyself remain true

Consider how the War on Drugs increases violence. The illegal drug economy overburdens our judicial system, increases prosecutorial workloads, and drives down homicide

clearance rates, leading to a phase shift in levels of violence
in urban areas. Then, as violence in urban contexts increases,
impoverished communities are ever more entrapped in the
protection rackets run by the gangs claiming to protect their
turf and the international traffickers who employ them. Imagine what liberation might look like.

> *I celebrate my folks died so I can be free*
> *Love and peace to any struggling incarcerated minority*

When in the course of human events, misguided laws have
resulted in the entrapment of a population in the jaws of ever-
more-powerful pirates, it becomes necessary to overthrow the
parastate, in the worst-case scenario, which we now face, by
legalizing it. Legalizing marijuana alone will not be enough
to dismantle the parastate. We have to set our faces squarely
to the future and learn how to decriminalize harder drugs as
well.

> *I bleed tears directly from my veins*
> *I cry for joy cause a future awaits w/o pain*

This has been done before. In 2001, Portugal eliminated
criminal penalties for low-level possession and consumption
of all illicit drugs and reclassified these activities as administrative violations. Instead of being arrested, people found in possession of personal-use amounts are ordered to appear before
a "dissuasion commission"; the result is treatment, a fine, or
other administrative sanctions. In contrast, drug trafficking

remains criminal. Yet decriminalization of personal-use possession has brought drug dependency out of the shadows. In Portugal, the number of people seeking treatment increased by 60 percent between 1998 and 2011, and adolescent drug use has decreased since the law's passage. At the same time, the percentage of people in Portugal's prisons for drug violations fell from 44 percent in 1999 to 24 percent in 2013. And the overall quantity of illicit drugs seized actually increased, possibly because public safety resources could be directed to targets higher up the supply chain.

Is parenting easier in this environment? No one's done that study, but a reduction in secrecy must surely be a boon, and having fewer children in jail cells, fewer prison visits to make, must lift morale.

> *All night my mother be praying on bended knees*
> *Symbolizing Harriet crawling till her knees bleed*
> *I plea to my b's & c's quit busting on each other*
> *Vision the pain that those who died sustained*
> *Imagine being split open and at your feet rests your brain*
> *Am I crazy? No I speak reality.*
> *From day to day livin' was a fight for liberty.*
> *So I thank Christ cause somebody prayed for me*
> *And you too, cause you're right here listening to me.*

Does legalizing marijuana everywhere and decriminalizing hard drugs sound like turning the world upside down? Here's what's been turned upside down. This girl who always tried to be squeaky clean—because she thought it was the only way to be safe—has turned into a proponent of legalizing drugs, including even decriminalizing heroin. Even though she's seen relatives ruined not just by incarceration but by addiction, too. I have become a legalizer. How about you?

Each one of us has the job of, somehow, absorbing the damage done to us as children and transmuting it into wisdom so that we do not pass it on. The terrible thing is that we have to achieve that transmutation before we have any wisdom, because the time to achieve this is between the ages of eleven and sixteen, when, like Michael, we choose our life course. It is not that by then we will know, or need to know, precisely what we will do in life but that by then we will have chosen how we are putting the basic building blocks together. What kinds of people will we want to live with? Can we delay gratification? Are our purposes pure? Will we live inside or outside of the law? Before we choose our building blocks, before we are fourteen or sixteen, perhaps, we need to transmute the damage done to us into wisdom. How many of us can do this? The more the damage that has been inflicted on a kid, the harder the job of transmutation, but even when there's not so much damage, I think none of us manages to transmute all of it, whatever the quantity it may be our particular burden to transmute. The question is mainly whether we've been given a light load or a heavy one. And if our burden is heavy, there is one more question. Can we transmute enough of the damage to survive? This is possible only if we ready ourselves to damage others less than we ourselves were damaged. This is the paradox: to save ourselves we have to prepare to save others by seeking to understand what went wrong with us.

Now I lay me down to sleep
And every morning I wake-up I think about this
     Juneteenth.

As a society, our challenge is the same. Can we damage the generations to come less than we ourselves were damaged? From the ground we stand on, we must understand the harm that has been done and ascertain how we can rebuild the foundation while we stand on it, so that we do not pass on the harm. The failed War on Drugs is something rotten. Its effects are by no means limited to those who sell or use.

Forgive us our trespasses
As we forgive those who trespass against us.

NOTES

PART I: RELEASE AND RESURRECTION

1 **Limits are:** from Charles Olson, "Letter Five," *Maximus* (Oakland: University of California Press, 1985).

CHAPTER 3: THE INVESTIGATION, JULY 2009

10 **Headline No. 1, from KTLA:** "a body riddled with bullets," KTLA News website, July 18, 2009, 9:39 PM PDT.

11 **Los Angeles Police Department blog:** "Man Found Dead in Car," July 20, 2009, available at http://lapdblog.typepad.com/ lapd_blog/2009/07/page/3/.

CHAPTER 8: FUNERAL, JULY 27, 2009

33 **The great grounding:** Frank Bidart, "You Cannot Rest," in *Watching the Spring Festival* (New York: Farrar, Straus & Giroux, 2009).

CHAPTER 11: THE END, AUGUST 2008–JULY 2009

50 **"I hate and I love":** "Catullus 85," trans. F. W. Cornish. Catullus and Tibullus, *Catullus. Tibullus. Pervigilium Veneris,* trans. F. W.

Cornish, J. P. Postgate, J. W. Mackail, rev. G. P. Goold, Loeb Classical Library 6 (Cambridge: Harvard University Press, 1913).

52 **The theologian Augustine captured her experience:** Augustine, *City of God*, Book 19, chap. 8.

56 **"arrow flew, as if of itself":** From Frank Bidart, "Fourth Hour of the Night." Preceding lines are "How each child finds that it must deal with/the intolerable//becomes its fate."

CHAPTER 12: CRIME AND PUNISHMENT

62 **To quote Atul Gawande:** Atul Gawande, *Being Mortal: Medicine and What Matters in the End* (New York: Metropolitan Books, 2014).

62 **time without "milestones":** William Muth and Ginger Walker, "Looking Up: The Temporal Horizons of a Father in Prison," in *Fathering* 11, no. 3 (Fall 2013): 292–305.

63 **"gaping abyss":** Fabrice Guilbaud, "Working in Prison: Time as Experienced by Inmate-Workers," in *Revue française de sociologie*: English issue. Vol. 51 (2010): 41–68.

CHAPTER 13: WHERE WAS OUR FAMILY? WHERE WERE THE LAWYERS?

74 **carjackings had nearly doubled:** "Governor Signs Death Penalty in Carjack Killings," *Daily Breeze* (Torrance, CA), September 27, 1995.

79 **"God causes all things to work":** Romans 8:28.

CHAPTER 15: NORCO

96 **YOU MIGHT WANT TO SEND HIM:** 2008 Blog Post at Prisontalk.com. Available at http://www.prisontalk.com/forums/showthread.php?t=350459.

CHAPTER 17: VISITING 1.0

109 *I always dress up like*: 2005 Blog Posts at Prisontalk.com. Available at http://www.prisontalk.com/forums/archive/index.php/t=408777.html.

110 *I must say I agree with Hisprettygirl*: Ibid.

CHAPTER 20: THE BIGGEST WILDFIRE IN CALIFORNIA HISTORY

142 **The more formal 99-page:** Jack Blackwell and Andrea Tuttle, "California Fire Siege 2003: The Story," U.S. Forest Service and California Department of Forestry, n.d.

CHAPTER 21: FIRE AND ICE

151 **The economists Claudia Goldin and Larry Katz:** In *The Race Between Education and Technology* (Cambridge: Harvard University Press, 2008).

151 **Some say the world:** Robert Frost, "Fire and Ice," in *Harper's Magazine* (1920).

CHAPTER 22: THE SINGLE MOTHER AND THE GREAT WHITE WHALE

154 **The number of black nurses:** In Michael Javen Fortner, *Black Silent Majority: The Rockefeller Drug Laws and the Politics of Punishment* (Kindle locations 737-738) (Cambridge: Harvard University Press, 2015). Kindle ed.

CHAPTER 24: "SIS, RUN!"

161 **no looting, arson, or damage during the Watts riots:** Jon Schleuss, "Inside the Watts Curfew Zone," *Los Angeles Times*,

August 11, 2015, http://graphics.latimes.com/watts-riots-1965
-map/.

161 **modern peak in ridership:** Wendell Cox, "Transit in Los
Angeles," *NewGeography Blog*, April 7, 2010, http://www.new
geography.com/content/001495-transit-los-angeles.

169 **from 9 percent to 25 percent:** Cheryl L. Maxson, "Street
Gangs and Drug Sales in Two Suburban Cities," *NIJ Research in
Brief*, September 1995, https://www.ncjrs.gov/txtfiles/strtgang
.txt.

169 **"the [annual] number of gang related homicides":** Randall
G. Shelden, Sharon K. Tracy, and William B. Brown, *Youth
Gangs in American Society* (Cengage, 2013), p. 115.

169 **"either jacked for money or you sold dope":** Sanyika Shakur
(aka Kody Scott), *Monster: The Autobiography of an L.A. Gang
Member* (New York: Grove/Atlantic, 2004), p. 251.

169 **"working was considered weak":** Ibid.

CHAPTER 25: GANGBANGING—A DEFINITION

172 **white-on-black race riots flared:** Robert A. Gibson, "The
Negro Holocaust: Lynching and Race Riots in the United
States, 1880–1950," Yale-New Haven Teacher Institute, Cur-
riculum Unit 79.02.04. Available at http://teachersinstitute.yale
.edu/curriculum/units/1979/2/79.02.04.x.html#c.

173 **Further domino effect riots against Latinos:** See Himilce
Novas, *Everything You Need to Know About Latino History* (New
York: Plume, 2008), p. 98.

173 **"The leaders of the [Catholic] Church":** From an oral history posted by a blogger, under the alias "Lonewolf." "White
Fence," on the *Brown Kingdom* blog, December 11, 2015,
http://13radicalriders14.blogspot.com/2015/12/white-fence.
html. The blog is not, in other words, a verified source of precisely how gangs developed, but it does capture people's percep-
tions of how they developed.

173 **"a lot of racism and violence":** Ibid.

175 **evidence, they say, is "overwhelming":** Shelden, Tracy, and Brown, *Youth Gangs in American Society*, pp. 107–110. These scholars write: "Two theories have been offered to explain why the crime rate is higher among gang members (Kaufman, 2010). One theory is called the 'selection model.' According to this view, those most likely to join gangs are 'already predisposed toward delinquency and violence.' The other perspective is known as the 'facilitation model.' This view argues that 'gang members are no more disposed toward delinquency and violence than others are and would not contribute to higher crime rates if they did not join a gang. However, when they do join a gang, peer pressures promote their increased involvement in delinquency' (Kaufman, 2010). The overwhelming evidence gives support to the latter view." In support of this view, these scholars describe the following observed pattern: "The first arrest for gang members typically came *after* becoming a gang member. In fact, in each of the areas where the research was conducted, the pattern was as follows: The youths began hanging out with the gangs at around age 12 or 13, joined the gang around 6 to 12 months after (between ages 13 and 14); and incurred their first arrest at around age 14. Typically they experience their first arrest about six months *after* they join the gang [emphasis added]."

176 **By 1961, the number of addicts:** Fortner, *Black Silent Majority* (Kindle location 822).

176 **unemployment for African Americans spiraled:** Shelden, Tracy, and Brown, *Youth Gangs in American Society*, p. 11.

177 **Charles Green launched:** President's Commission on Organized Crime (Irving Kaufman, Chair), "Trafficking and Organized Crime," in *America's Habit: Drug Abuse, Drug Trafficking, and Organized Crime* (1986), chap. 3, part 1. Available at https://catalog.hathitrust.org/Record/001087693.

178 **"a community based organization":** Shelden, Tracy, and Brown, *Youth Gangs in American Society*, p. 13.

179 **a world of white distributors and independent distributors:** One can work out the distribution patterns for narcotics by studying the state-by-state "Drug Threat Assessment" documents that states submit to the National Drug Intelligence Center. See a 2002 example from Tennessee here: https://www.justice.gov/archive/ndic/pubs1/1017/cocaine .htm#Distribution. These state-by-state reports become the basis for a synthesized national drug threat assessment report put out by the Department of Justice and the Drug Enforcement Agency. For the 2016 report, see https://www.dea.gov/ resource-center/2016%20NDTA%20Summary.pdf.

179 **A study found that in Pasadena in 1995:** Cheryl L. Maxson, "Street Gangs and Drug Sales in Two Suburban Cities," in *NIJ Research in Brief*, September 1995. https://www.ncjrs.gov/txtfiles/ strtgang.txt. See also Shelden, Tracy, and Brown, *Youth Gangs*.

CHAPTER 27: THE LIMIT ON HELPING YOUR KIDS

191 **According to the report . . . 39.8 percent:** California Attorney General's Office, Crime and Violence Prevention Center, *Gangs: A Statewide Directory of Programs: Prevention, Intervention, Suppression* (Sacramento, 1994).

CHAPTER 28: CITY OF ANGELS

195 **Operation Pipeline:** The Drug Enforcement Administration addresses the history of Operation Pipeline on its website here: https://www.dea.gov/about/history/1980-1985.pdf. That history is also discussed in Michelle Alexander, *The New Jim Crow* (New York: New Press, 2010).

195 **what we have come to know as racial profiling:** David Kocieniewski, "New Jersey Argues that U.S. Wrote the Book on Racial Profiling," *New York Times*, November 29, 2000. See also Alexander, *The New Jim Crow*.

196 **From 1790 to 1950 the number of mandatory minimums:**
Naomi Murakawa. *The First Civil Right: How Liberals Built Prison America* (Studies in Postwar American Political Development) (Oxford University Press, 2014), p. 116.

196 **created its first gang database:** On gang databases, see Max Felker-Kantor, "Managing Marginalization from Watts to Rodney King: The Struggle over Policing and Social Control in Los Angeles, 1965–1992" (Ph.D. diss., University of Southern California, 2014), pp. 381–83. For statistics on nearly half of African American men in Los Angeles County under age twenty-five as gang members, see Nina Siegel, "Ganging Up on Civil Liberties," *Progressive* 61 (October 1997): 28–31.

196 **no fewer than 1,400 African American youth:** Donna Murch, "Crack in Los Angeles: Crisis, Militarization, and Black Response to the Late Twentieth-Century War on Drugs," *Journal of American History*, June 2015, p. 162–73.

196 **"the casual drug user":** Ronald J. Ostrow, "Casual Drug Users Should Be Shot, Gates Says," *Los Angeles Times,* September 6, 1990, p. A19. For Daryl F. Gates's argument for greater incarceration rates, see Felker-Kantor, "Managing Marginalization from Watts to Rodney King," 409–10.

196 The **African American prison population in California:** Murch, "Crack in Los Angeles," pp. 162–73.

198 **far more powerful system:** I wrote to a Stanford psychologist who works on the impact of a pressing sense of mortality on one's decision-making to ask her if she knew of any work on juvenile offenders and inmates and the effects of long sentences on their psyches. She wrote this back to me: "Dear Danielle, Nice to e-meet you. About 20 years ago my group began to explore relationships between time horizons and gang membership. The idea was prompted by reports that young men living in high crime neighborhoods did not expect to survive their 20s. I reasoned that gangs may represent highly selective and strong social bonds and reflect preferences similar to those of

elderly people for smaller and emotionally meaningful social relationships. We collected some survey data from a high school in a high crime neighborhood and findings supported the hypothesis about shortened time horizons in youth: Those who were in gangs or considering joining gangs had time horizons comparable to the elderly. Those who were the same age but not in or interested in gangs had much longer time horizons.

"I visited a youth incarceration 'camp' and spent a day talking with middle and high school aged boys who were in gangs. By the end of the day, I had given up the idea of studying the question. I learned from these boys that they had essentially no choice but to join a gang. Some told me that they didn't 'join' at all; they were simply default members by virtue of their addresses.

"If I'd had an idea of a way my research could have helped them, I would have pursued it. But because my question was theoretical and I saw no way it would be useful—given how overdetermined their situations seemed to be—I felt that it would be exploitative to pursue the research so I let it go. We never published these data.

"Your email prompted this memory. I don't know of any other research on the topic, published or unpublished."

199 **32 percent of defendant filings:** See Federal Judicial Caseload Statistics for 2013, available at http://www.uscourts.gov/statistics-reports/federal-judicial-caseload-statistics-2013.

199 **According to Vernon Geberth:** Interviewed by Martin Kaste for "Open Cases: Why One-Third of Murders in America Go Unresolved," *National Public Radio: Morning Edition*, March 30, 2015. Available at http://www.npr.org/2015/03/30/395069137/open-cases-why-one-third-of-murders-in-america-go-unresolved.

199 **the average clearance rate for homicide:** Ibid. See also Jill Leovy, *Ghettoside: A True Story of Murder in America* (New York: Spiegel & Grau), 2015.

199 **In contrast, in Detroit in the years:** Martin Kaste, "Open Cases: Why One-Third of Murders in America Go Unresolved," National Public Radio, *Morning Edition*, March 30, 2015.

199 **In Chicago in 2009:** Mark Konkol and Frank Main, "59 Hours," *Chicago Sun-Times,* July 5, 2010.

199 **hide the low rate of cases ending in arrest and prosecution:** Mike Reicher, "LAPD Closed Homicide Cases Without Bringing Killers to Justice, Analysis Shows," *Los Angeles Daily News*, January 24, 2015.

200 **Two economists, Brendan O'Flaherty and Rajiv Sethi:** Brendan O'Flaherty and Rajiv Sethi, "Homicide in Black and White," in *Journal of Urban Economics* 68, no. 3 (November 2010): 215–30.

202 **an estimated $100 billion on illegal narcotics:** Danielle Allen, "How the War on Drugs Creates Violence," *Washington Post*, October 16, 2015, citing Office of National Drug Control Policy, "What America's Users Spend on Illegal Drugs: 2000–2010," 2014. Available at https://www.whitehouse.gov/sites/default/files/ondcp/policy-and-research/wausid_results_report.pdf.

202 **the police had 47 percent of African American men:** Murch, "Crack in Los Angeles."

CODA: WHAT NEXT?

218 **One out of every one hundred adult Americans:** Committee on Causes and Consequences of High Rates of Incarceration, Committee on Law and Justice, Division of Behavioral and Social Sciences and Education, National Research Council, *The Growth of Incarceration in the United States: Exploring Causes and Consequences,* ed. Jeremy Travis, Bruce Western, and Steve Redburn (Washington D.C.: National Academies Press, 2014), p. 2.

219 **Twenty-five percent of the world's prisoners:** Ibid.

220 **In 2001, Portugal eliminated criminal penalties:** Drug Policy Alliance, "Drug Decriminalization in Portugal: A Health-Centered Approach," February 2015. Available at https://www.drugpolicy.org/sites/default/files/DPA_Fact_Sheet_Portugal_Decriminalization_Feb2015.pdf.

A NOTE ON SOURCES

I am grateful to my family, especially my aunt Karen; cousins Nicholas, Roslyn, and Pili; my father and mother, William Allen and Susan Allen; and my former husband and stepson Robert von Hallberg and Isaac von Hallberg for taking the time to share their memories with me, even over the course of repeated interviews and follow-up conversations. In order to reconstruct events, I depended not merely on their memories and my own, but also on articles about Michael's attempted carjacking in the *Daily Breeze* (Torrance, Calif.) and court records for Michael's case and Bree's later homicide and manslaughter case. Whereas most California court documents are available to the general public through the court archives, juvenile records are not. Despite the fact that he was treated as an adult, Michael's case was filed as a "Youth Authority" or juvenile case. Consequently, I have not been able to secure the whole of his record and was able to secure those parts that I did acquire access to only via formal public records requests. I am unlikely to have succeeded in that effort without the valuable legal advice of Joshua Milon. It is worth noting that, in California, the court files of juvenile defendants who reached the age of eighteen but are now deceased are orphan files. No one has a legal right to them. The defendant, who is deceased, cannot access them, of course. Neither, though, can their parents if the deceased passed the age of eighteen before passing away. Such was the situation with Michael's file. It was difficult, in the first instance, to find it, because it had been misfiled. Once I found the file, it was held up to me, through a glass partition, in its full thickness of several inches. The clerk then informed me that she would have to review it and remove anything marked confidential. After twenty minutes, she returned to me with a file with very little left in it. This is what led me down the path of making public record requests. I am extremely grateful for the material that I was able to secure, but I did not secure the whole of Michael's file. There are other mysteries in it that I may never be able to untangle, for instance a letter that Michael wrote in 2001 from prison to the judge who sentenced him.

ACKNOWLEDGMENTS

First and foremost, I must thank my friend and colleague, Henry Louis Gates, Jr., without whose invitation to give Harvard's DuBois Lectures, this book would never have been written. The purpose of those lectures is to contribute to our better understanding of African American life, history, and culture. As, over years, I contemplated giving those lectures, I could think of no topic more important than the ravages of mass incarceration. Yet that topic, that material was too hard, too personal. Without a firm date, a room booked and an audience expected, I'm not sure I would ever have been able to finish this.

Second, I thank my friend, Quiara Alegria Hudes, whose own public statement about a cousin, a chapter in my book *Education and Equality*, gave me the courage to start.

To my family, of course, I owe everything. My parents and brother, my grandparents, aunts, uncles, and cousins. My former husband and stepsons. My husband and children. All have in one way or another helped author this book.

My daughter, Nora, came across me one evening at work with photos of Michael spread out.

Who is that, she wanted to know?

"It's Michael."

"Who is Michael?" she said.

Well, Nora, this is Michael.

If the material was hard for me, it was excruciating for my aunt Karen and cousins Nicholas and Roslyn, who endured repeated interviews and my insistent, continuous prob-ing. Each of us had been seeking understanding, and peace, through a solitary journey. Never had we tried to assemble our story together. While the process has been painful, I believe we have all achieved greater clarity. By and by, we have come to understand, at least in part, and this can put some of our incessant mourning to rest, I hope.

My agent, Tina Bennett, my editor, Bob Weil, and miracle-working assistant Emily Bromley are stalwart friends, advo-cates, and teachers. They believe in me, and we should all be so lucky to have their sort of fierce support.

Many, many more assisted, too, of course. My friends and colleagues at Harvard's Edmond J. Safra Center for Eth-ics, in the Government Department and Graduate School of Education, in the Hutchins Center for African and African American Research, in the Department of African and Afri-can American Studies. My students across campus, of course. And all of the extraordinary scholars and writers—people like Bruce Western, Elizabeth Hinton, Glenn Loury, Rajiv Sethi, Tommie Shelby, Brandon Terry, Michael Fortner, Michelle Alexander, Jill Leovy—and so many others who have at last opened up the story of mass incarceration so that we may all consider our circumstances with clear eyes.

Also, this story could never have been written without able

and generous legal work by Joshua Milon, without the courteous and sympathetic assistance of staff in the Los Angeles courts archives and records offices, without the smiling help of staff in several branches of the Los Angeles County library system, and without the patient responsiveness of Irene Wakabayashi, in the District Attorney's Office, who fielded my multiple public records requests.

I am also grateful to all the people at Norton and Liveright who have helped make this book possible, especially Peter Miller, Cordelia Calvert, and Marie Pantojan.

Finally, I want to say thank you to the many people who came up to me after I relayed Michael's story for the first time, in those DuBois Lectures, and said, I, too, love someone who is in prison or I, too, have lost someone to the ravages of the world of drugs. So many people shared their own painful stories with me. You, too, are in my heart's locket.

CREDITS

TEXT

10 Headline No. 1, from KTLA: "A body riddled with bullets," KTLA News website, July 18, 2009, 9:39 PM PDT. Reprinted courtesy of KTLA.

33 Excerpt from "You Cannot Rest," from *Watching the Spring Festival* by Frank Bidart. Copyright © 2008 by Frank Bidart. Reprinted by permission of Farrar, Straus and Giroux.

56 "arrow flew, as if of itself": From Frank Bidart, "The Fourth Hour of the Night," from *Half-Light: Collected Poems 1965–2016* by Frank Bidart. Copyright © 2017 by Frank Bidart. Reprintd by permission of Farrar, Straus and Giroux.

57 Expert quoted by the *Los Angeles Times*, Sept. 6, 1995, "New Wave of Mayhem; Juveniles Are Increasingly Committing Violent Crimes—and Experts Don't Know Why or How Best to Stop Them." Reprinted with permission of quoted expert.

174 Excerpt from "Jet Song," from *West Side Story* by Leonard Bernstein and Stephen Sondheim. © Copyright 1956, 1957, 1958, 1959 by Amberson Holdings LLC and Stephen Sondheim. Copyright renewed. Leonard Bernstein Music Publishing Company LLC, publisher. Boosey & Hawkes, agent for rental. International copyright secured.

IMAGES

14 Photo of Michael from Danielle's wedding. Photo by Laura Slatkin.

23 The author and her cousin, Michael, at her wedding. Photo by Sharon Renee Hartley.

28 The entrance to Los Angeles Valley Community College. Photo courtesy of Isaac Van Hallberg.

48 Michael Allen, in Central Juvenile, with mother, Karen Allen, autumn 1995. Photo by California Youth Authority.

48 Michael Allen in California Rehabilitation Center–Norco, date uncertain. Photo by California Youth Authority.

48 Michael Allen in California Rehabilitation Center–Norco, date uncertain. Photo by California Youth Authority.

48 Michael and Karen Allen, Visiting Day in California Rehabilitation Center–Norco, 2004. Photo by California Youth Authority.

49 Michael Allen, during second phase in prison, 2007–2008. Photo by California Youth Authority.

84 Michael in Centinela, on prayer rug. California Youth Authority.

86 Map of places where Michael was incarcerated. Map created by Anna Oler.

87 "Norco, CA State Prison," 2015, photo by Stephen Tourlentes, courtesy of Carroll and Sons Gallery, Boston, MA.

96 "Chino, CA State Prison, 2015," photo by Stephen Tourlentes, courtesy of Carroll and Sons Gallery, Boston, MA.

100 Elizabeth Eckford turning away from hostile crowds outside of Central High School in Little Rock, Arkansas, Sept. 4, 1957. Bettmann/Getty Images.

108 Aerial photo of California Rehabilitation Center–Norco. Courtesy of the California Department of Corrections and Rehabilitation.

126 Fire burns above the city of San Diego. Photo included in U.S.

and California governmental report, "The Story: California Fire Siege 2003." Courtesy of CAL FIRE Archives.

136 Fire burns along a hill line endangering homes. Courtesy of CAL FIRE Archives.

154 Newborn. Photo courtesy of Karen Allen.

158 First steps. Photo courtesy of Karen Allen.

164 Childhood. Photos courtesy of Karen Allen.

166 Kindergarten graduation. Photos courtesy of Karen Allen.

168 Michael on the hillside sidewalk where he crashed his bike. Photo courtesy of Karen Allen.

190 Michael on a junior high school football team. Photo courtesy of Karen Allen.

Danielle Allen is James Bryant Conant University Professor at Harvard University and director of Harvard's Edmond J. Safra Center for Ethics. She is a political philosopher widely known for her work on justice and citizenship in both ancient Athens and modern America as well as a contributing columnist for the *Washington Post*. She lives in Cambridge, Massachusetts, with her husband and two children.